A LEGACY OF SUCCESSFUL

BUSINESS PRACTICES

A Modern Day Business Boot Camp

For Owners and Managers

By

Dr. James A. McCain
The Business Doctor

Thirty Years Helping Small

And Midsized Businesses

Survive and Prosper

ISBN: 978-1-84961-153-4

Published by: RealTime Publishing

Limerick, Ireland

TABLE OF CONTENTS

Note to Readers Page 8

**Forward: Turning Good Businesses into
Better Businesses** Page 9
Why I wrote this book and how it can help businesses succeed
and flourish.

Chapter One: Lean Toward Fundamentals Page 13

Why fundamental business practices, not esoteric
methodologies, determine the success or failure of small to
midsized businesses. This chapter is, in essence, the theme of
this book.

Chapter Two: Apply Critical Task Thinking Page 20

Basic tasks that determine your success or failure:
>Work smart
>Manage cash flow
>Establish collegial relationships and exchanges of
>>information among peers
>Assure that education for managers and employees is
>>practical and focused
>Continually improve product and service value and
>>reduce waste
>Do not micro manage
>Maintain compliance to regulatory requirements

Chapter Three: Articulate the Company's Mission Statement Page 30

Articulating the company's mission keeps all managerial eyes focused on the job ahead. This chapter shows how to construct a mission statement based on the purpose and objectives of the business.

   The mission statement explained
   Questions to ask before formulating a mission statement
   Discover important information you want included in
      your mission statement

Chapter Four: Develop an Organization Structure to Match the Mission Statement Page 35
List of functions for organization structure
Position titles and organization structure
         Position titles
         Organization structure
Summary of core tasks

Chapter Five: Construct a Business Plan Page 49
Do you know where you are going?
Business plan analysis
Develop the business action plan (BAP)
Business review checklist
Business planning synopsis

Chapter Six: Create a Financial Plan to Match the Business Plan Page 67
Financial plan format
Operating ratios
Breakeven analysis
Financial back-up information

Chapter Seven: Finance Your Business Page 74
Narrowing the search for funds
Self funding
Locating private resources

Chapter Eight: Apply Responsive Accounting Procedures Page 90
Balance sheet
      Assets
      Liabilities
      Stockholder's equity
P&L statement
Income (revenues)
Cost of sales
Operating expenses (overhead)
Other income/expenses
Taxes on income

Chapter Nine: Control Overhead Page 101
Overhead expense accumulation
Overhead application formulas
Overhead and under-absorbed overhead

Chapter Ten: Calculate Variances to Plan and Take Corrective Action Page 109
Calculate variances to plan
Corrective action mode
Variance corrective action plan

Chapter Eleven: Improve Productivity Page 120
Labor productivity
Sales productivity
Employee teams

Chapter Twelve: Manage Employee Wages and Wage Expectations Page 133
Basic concepts about wages and employee wage expectations
Wage management and budget control
Procedures for awarding merit increases
Salary ranges
Employee motivation: money vs. non-monetary rewards

Chapter Thirteen: Install Timely and Effective Purchasing Procedures Page 145
Supply chain management
Negotiating prices and delivery dates
Monthly and annual physical inventory

Chapter Fourteen: Control and Reduce Inventory Page 153
ABC analysis
Minimum/maximum inventory procedure

Chapter Fifteen: Manage Production Planning and Scheduling Page161
Definition of planning and scheduling terms
Production unit capacity
The scheduling process
Job schedule
Production scheduling procedure for a gun manufacturer

Chapter Sixteen: Cut Rejects and Improve Customer Satisfaction through ISO Quality standards Page 169
Quality planning
Document and data control
Product identification and traceability
Process control
Inspection and testing
Control of non-conforming product
Handling, storage, packaging, preservation, and delivery

Chapter Seventeen: Install a Responsive Human Resources Function Page 180
Employee relations
Labor relations
Training coordinator

Chapter Eighteen: Penetrate Markets and Raise Sales Levels Page 194
Marketing analysis
Developing a sales and marketing plan
Typical sales and marketing plan
Sample sales and marketing plan work sheet

Chapter Nineteen: Analyze Your Business Page 216
Money
Activities
Employees
Sales
Self-assessment

Chapter Twenty: Prepare a Succession Plan Page 230
Prepare a succession plan
Choosing your successor
Be prepared
Heir apparent
Recruiting from the outside
Training your successor

Appendix Page 241
Sample mission statements
Summary of terms used in MAPS
Summary of author and his last book

NOTE TO READERS

On the following pages you are going to read many practical, hands-on methods and procedures for improving every aspect of your business. In several instances you will see company names such as ABC, Inc. or ABC International. These are fictional companies designed to show you how the procedures described in this book work in a successful small or midsized business (as are the names of people used in the book). Please keep in mind that these are *representative* methods and procedures for the *typical* company. But since the size and scope of company operations for small and midsized businesses vary immensely, you will need to tailor the solutions shown for your specific company.

If you have any questions about applying these methods and procedures, please do not hesitate to contact me via my email address mccain97@aol.com.

Thanks and best of luck,
Jim McCain

FORWARD AND ACKNOWLEDGEMENTS

Turning Business Failures
Into Business Successes

Why I Wrote This Book and How It Can
Help Businesses Succeed and Flourish

With the economy stalled and prices for parts and materials increasing, the importance of doing the right things and doing them at the right time is assuming even greater importance than normally. When the economy is booming and orders are pouring in, the sheer amount of sales dollars can—and often does—cover up mistakes and bad business decisions.

No longer. Shrinking sales dollars and profit margins put a strain especially on small and midsized businesses struggling simply to stay alive. Under these dire circumstances, understanding how to control costs and stay on schedule producing high quality products and services is paramount.

That's where I come in. My name is Jim McCain. For the 30 years I've spent helping companies regain or strengthen profitability, I have come to recognize one pervasive truth: business owners and managers don't focus on business fundamentals because they're often too involved with the technical nuts and bolts of their companies. They are so busy working *in* their business that they have little time to work *on* their business.

Businesspeople often recognize problems, but many don't understand how or why the problems happened or how to fix them. Some run out of cash, some fall behind customer delivery promises, some don't realize they have too many or too few workers before they run out of money or miss scheduled completion dates, some don't understand the critical nature of quality control and customer service, some don't know how to properly account for expenditures. I could go on and on; the list of business-related problems is virtually endless.

Not that small and midsized company owners and managers are unique when it comes to business problems; they certainly aren't. Even the largest commercial companies exhibit the same problems mentioned here. The difference is that the larger companies have the luxury of hiring specialists to fix business problems. Smaller companies, many of them operating on shoestring budgets, can't afford to employ full-time specialists in finance, accounting, inventory control, scheduling, quality, productivity, cost control, and the many other specialties that often spell the difference between success and failure of a commercial enterprise.

And quite often, forces beyond their control compound their problems. For example, a faltering economy, extravagant union demands, inflation, and parts and material shortages. All of these, and more, play a role and tend to exasperate the small and midsized companies' struggle to keep their heads above water.

Many turn to management books. While the bookstores are crammed full of business advice for companies of all sizes, large and small, more often than not theoreticians write them, and they're the worst possible advisors because they have no direct experience running a business. Academic advice will take you only so far; as the saying goes, theory doesn't cut it on the firing line.

Practical businesspeople get impatient with such books that teach theory and those that contain endless lists of so-called sophisticated business methods and techniques that take a Philadelphia lawyer to interpret. Learning from such books is not their bag (nor mine). *But a book that shows small and midsized company owners and managers how to repair deficient parts of their business, spoken in the language they understand, gets their attention.* And that's the secret of my method and the focus of this book. I show such businesspeople how to address problems and strengthen their companies, and I never throw academic lessons at them or inundate them with business theory. Indeed, I've lived every last word of advice I give in this book. I learned my lessons right on the firing line so I know what works and what doesn't.

I have been blessed with many friends, family members and associates who have helped me through all of these countless and wonderful experiences. I can name only a few here.

I thank the many hundreds of business owners who trusted me and allowed me to enter, improve and share the joy of their business experiences.

I thank my mentors, colleagues, students and critics for their devoted attention to my work and allowing me to give mine to theirs.

I thank my brilliant and creative staff executives and senior consultants who labored many difficult hours with me often under unusual circumstances, to execute the numerous directives, program initiatives and details outlined in my scopes of work. Their loyalty, integrity, good judgment, common sense and hard work brought change and success to many business owners.

I thank my friends at Legacy Analytics Ltd., and many other quality consulting organizations, who have made this journey a real pleasure.

Finally, I thank my wife, Elaine, who for years has lovingly allowed me to pursue my work while patiently enduring my lengthy absences. Her selfless and unconditional support for my ventures has been essential to their accomplishment.

CHAPTER ONE

Lean Toward Fundamentals

Why Fundamental Business Practices, Not Esoteric Methodologies, Determine the Success or Failure of Small and Midsized Businesses.

The title of this chapter is, in essence, the theme of this book. Let me start by telling you a story about Mike, a former business client of mine, the CEO of a midsized manufacturer. At the early stages of his career he was inventory control manager for a construction equipment manufacturer in the South. His company was installing a new computerized MRP (material requirements planning system), a sophisticated and often complex undertaking that uses advanced software to manage inventory levels, production flow, and customer delivery schedules.

Early results of the system installation were disappointing, to say the least. Conversion from the former manual system to the new computerized MRP system caused disruption of work flows throughout the plant while inventory levels surged—two dangerous signs pointing to swollen costs and missed customer delivery promises. Both of them kisses of death to a manufacturing company.

The manufacturing plant bought many of its parts and supplies from vendors stretched across the USA and in Europe. One of its suppliers, a manufacturer of small castings in Sweden, had a record of never missing a customer delivery due date while operating with a low inventory level that put other manufacturing companies to shame.

The equipment manufacturing company's vice president of manufacturing decided to find out what the supplier's secret was. He sent Mike to Sweden to find out.

Mike, a young man at the time, was brimming with new ideas and eager to implement them. It had been his enthusiasm about the new MRP system and his ability to sell it to his company's top executives that had been behind the company's decision to buy the very expensive MRP system from a consulting firm.

The young manager flew over to Sweden on a Saturday night, rested on Sunday, and reported to the foundry owner bright and early Monday morning. I am reproducing the ensuing conversation as best I can from my recollection of what Mike told me many years later:

I wasn't impressed with the owner's office. It was on the second story of the foundry and furnished with beat-up old metal furniture. Foundry dust from the castings ground in the factory below had sifted up and coated every square inch of the owner's office.

In fact I wasn't impressed with the factory owner. He was an older man with graying hair and a slight stoop to his shoulders. He was dressed in dirty jeans, a wrinkled denim shirt he wore with its sleeves rolled up, and a pair of clumsy looking safety shoes.

By contrast, I had dressed for the visit. I tried to keep my immaculate Brooks Brothers suit from getting dirty, and I brushed off a chair before sitting down and facing the factory owner. Bjorn, the owner, noticed and smiled at me. "I should have warned you about the foundry environment," he said. "Dirty clothes are the norm."

"I don't speak Swedish," I said, while shaking off foundry dust from my jacket.

"That's okay," Bjorn said in a thick Swedish accent. "I speak good English."

The two exchanged pleasantries for a few minutes, and then Bjorn got down to business.

"I understand you want to know more about our inventory control system."

I nodded. "Your inventory turnover[1] record is incredible. Twelve turns. Wow!"

Bjorn smiled. "Thank you."

"And you never miss a scheduled customer shipment. Very impressive."

"Well," Bjorn said, "that's not quite true. Last year during the shipping strike we missed two shipping dates. But you're right, overall we stay on schedule. We consider that paramount, along with keeping inventory levels low and moving castings quickly through the factory."

Mike leaned back in his chair. "I guess the question is: How do you do it? How do you maintain that high turnover rate?"

"Keeping minimum inventory on hand comes down to knowing when to reorder."

"May I take a look at your MRP system?"

Bjorn smiled again. "We don't have an MRP system."

---

[1] An accounting term signifying the number of times inventory is sold during the year. The larger the turnover rate, the lower the inventory cost.

"What?" Mike looked dumbstruck.

"In fact we don't use any computers at all for production planning. The only person who uses one is our controller and accounting manager."

"I don't get it. How do you maintain that high turnover rate? How do you control your inventories?"

A sly smile crept across Bjorn's face. He stood and faced a window of his office overlooking a silo in back of the property. "Come here," he motioned to me.

I rose from my chair and joined Bjorn at the window.

"Take a look at that silo. What do you see?"

I peered at the silo. "I see a large silo with an elongated window on its side near the top and a moving conveyor belt leading to the top of the silo."

"What's the conveyor belt carrying?"

"Looks like castings."

"And what do you see in the window of the silo?"

"Same thing. Looks like castings."

Bjorn smiled. "Exactly! That's what they are. When we make the raw castings we store them in the silo and later remove them from a chute in the bottom, grind off the parting lines[2], package and ship them to your company and others."

Mike looked puzzled. "I don't get it. What's that got to do with your inventory control system?"

This time, Bjorn beamed at Mike. "That is out inventory control system. When the castings drop below the window of the silo I know it's time to order another batch through the foundry. That's our system."

---

[2] Lines on the castings made from the casting dies.

Okay, blame me for citing a simplistic example of the necessity of avoiding complexity. But the example does drive home the point. Simple is best: Easy-to-understand, easy-to-apply systems work. Employees respond well because they grasp how to use them readily.

Yes, there will always be a need for higher evolved, more complex, systems such as MRP. But my point is why not work with the simplest systems available provided they meet your needs? Simple systems translate to lower costs, higher productivity, and more dollars for the bottom line. And it doesn't make any difference if you're selling a product or a service. The foundry owner knew what he had to do to keep inventories low while maintaining customer delivery schedules, and he did it at the lowest possible cost. He had discovered what so many other managers miss, and that leads to the first of the many McCain's Maxims you will find in this book:

McCain's Maxim #1: Apply the simplest system available that will do the job. If you're unsure, start with what's easiest for your employees to understand and work with, then move it up a level of complexity if it does not meet your expectations. At some point you will find the optimal system: where costs are lowest relative to what works for your organization. *At that point, leave it alone.*

Mike returned to the USA with a new perspective and appreciation for doing things the easiest way possible. The first thing he did was to temporarily suspend using the MRP software and revert to a manual MRP system until the company worked out the kinks. Eventually, after achieving the company's inventory turnover and delivery goals, was he able to reinstall the computerized MRP system and drive inventory costs even further down.

In another example, one of the country's major automotive companies experimented with applying statistical process control (SPC) on one of its subassembly lines. The concept of using SPC is a good one; you cannot fault the job it does to keep defects and scrap low and output quality high.

Yet it failed because both managers and workers didn't understand it. The science of statistics was beyond their knowledge and interests, and its application was unduly complex. It wasn't until later years, when the company rolled out an automated self-correcting SPC system was the application successful. In this case, managers and workers didn't have to grasp statistical theory and apply complex statistical principles. The automated SPC system made corrections to the process itself. Simplicity was restored along with high levels of assembly quality.

It strikes me that some company owners and managers opt for what is most sophisticated at the expense of what works best. That's often the case with top executives who want bragging rights at the country club. CEO Jimmy brags to CEO Tom that his company is applying the very latest in just-in-time methods.CEO Jimmy may not really understand just-in-time methodology, but he knows it's "in" because the business press is chock full of stories of companies that do, *along with the pictures of those companies' CEOs.*

The same disease pervades some corporate boardrooms of companies that are experiencing problems meeting their financial goals, and turn to sophisticated methods to rescue them. This seldom works, because whatever got them in trouble the first place is almost always related to fundamentals: poor or inexperienced management, lack of basic systems in place, lack of attention to detail, and a host of other rudiments. It's comparable to a football team that has drifted away from run, block, and tackle executions to fancy plays such as reverses, halfback passes, and wildcat formations. Many times those plays compensate for weaknesses in the team. Which leads to another McCain's Maxim?

McCain's Maxim #2: Sophisticated solutions rarely solve business problems. For example, the most advanced analytical tool devised won't improve productivity or throughput if workers are unskilled or poorly trained (more often than not, the root cause of the problem). Owners and managers facing such difficult problems should turn their attention to fundamentals, much as when a new NFL coach retrains his players in blocking and tackling.

CHAPTER TWO

Apply Critical Task Thinking

Basic Tasks That Determine Your Success or Failure

An inevitable question that all company executives face is what basic tasks are ground floor requirements in today's challenging business environment and which ones just cause clutter and confusion? It's not as easy to determine as you would think. Sure, if you're running a manufacturing company you need production, inventory control, and shipping. Or, if you have a service business you need services that support selling and delivering the service. But over and beyond that, what other functions do owners, managers, and their employees need that are central to making a profit? And, just as important, what functions are just a distraction or, worse, damaging? I call this critical task thinking.

Let's examine a mix of both. From this we can evolve a guiding maxim.

Work Smart

Average business people feel comfortable working about 2500 hours per year (50 hours per week for 50 weeks, allowing for two weeks of vacation). This represents the total number of hours worked including all tasks. Yet, in a small business or midsized company, most owners and managers have difficulty wooing potential customers three hours a day out of the 10 hours at work. The reason is a seemingly endless supply of non-selling distractions with which business people in large companies don't have to deal.

By the end of the day, they know they have been working hard, but have no idea why they only worked on revenue generating items for three hours out of the ten. This is a common problem faced by businesspeople in small and midsized businesses who are working hard but not working smart.

Here's how you can work smarter: The key to getting control of your day is to set clear priorities. Make a list of common activities in which you engage daily (including all the non-revenue distractions) and prioritize that list according to importance. Revenue generators and marketing your business will be at the top of this list.

After you construct a good general priority list, you have a template for prioritizing your activities. Divide the tasks into four categories according to urgency and importance.

Category One (Important & Urgent) - In this category you should put tasks that are critical to your business, where time deadlines have passed or are imminent. These items are top priority. You should work almost exclusively on these items until this box is empty. Examples would be paying the rent, preparing for tomorrow's important decision-making meeting, completing an order before time runs out, preparing an order or a document you promised for a customer, calling a customer who is threatening to fire you. This is the fire-fighting box. The more items in here, the more harried and stressed you will be, and the more your work will suffer. If you are running your business effectively, this box should be nearly empty.

Category Two (Important But Not Urgent) - In this category you should put tasks that are critical to your business where deadlines are not looming. These items are your second priority after completing category one. Most of your important matters should reside in this box. Your daily objective is to get items in this box completed before they reach a point where they belong in category one.

Category Three (Urgent But Not Important) - Here you put items that are screaming for attention, but are not critical to your business. Telephone calls from friends and family that are not bona fide emergencies should wait until you are home or until you have completely run out of items in the first two groups. Computer related projects that are not critical to your ability to do projects in category one and two (like organizing your files) need to wait for a time when those two boxes are empty. These are discretionary tasks. They are distractions. Resist the urge to act on them until you complete important matters.

Category Four (Not Urgent and Not Important) - These are utter distractions and time wasters. They are allies in refining your procrastination skills and will destroy your productivity. They include things like reading newspapers and periodicals, surfing the Net, calling family and friends who haven't called you in a while, talking about college football with a friend or your partner for 40 minutes, going shopping for personal items. This is the money-sucking zone. You need to do these on personal time. They have no place cluttering up your day.

After you have completed your initial priority lists, you are ready to begin attacking your work. The tasks with top priority will be those in category one. Within that group, prioritize the tasks by which items have the greatest combination of importance and urgency. When you finish this group, begin working on category two, and so on.

At the beginning of each day, you should update the lists. Certain category one projects will be complete and thus crossed off the list. Add new items to your lists each day. This exercise might take 15 to 20 minutes each day, but it will improve your productivity by one to two hours daily, and that's a lot of time recaptured.

Manage Cash Flow

Every company must manage its cash flow or it will soon be out of business. Many businesspeople make the mistake of equating cash flow with profits; they are not the same thing. A company can be highly profitable and go out of business because it is starved for cash. This is particularly true when a company is growing rapidly and its need for purchased parts and materials outstrips its intake of cash from sales. Given that most companies quote thirty days net for its customers aggravates the problem because with a growing order bank they have an increasing need for purchased parts and materials but may not be generating the cash to pay for them.

The objective of preparing a cash flow projection is to determine deficiencies or excesses in the cash position which is necessary to operate the business, during the time for which the projection is prepared. If deficiencies are revealed in the cash flow, financial plans must be altered to increase cash by injecting more equity or capital through getting a loan, increasing prices, or reducing expenditures.

In cases of excess cash, it might indicate excessive borrowing or idle money that could be put to work. The objective of cash management is to implement a plan which will provide a well-managed flow of cash.

The preparation and maintenance of a cash flow forecast projection requires some time and effort, but the advantage of completing the forecast far outweighs the effort required.

Cash flow forecasts are more precise over a short term, becoming less precise as they are pushed further into the future. For this reason, the best results are obtained by making frequent short term forecasts rather than long range forecasts. The forecast suggested here projects into six weeks. As a week is completed and actual results are entered, an additional week is projected, maintaining six weeks of projected cash flow. Owners can adjust the length of time over which the forecast is operable length of time over which the forecast is operable to encompass the period desired, including as much as one year prepared on some computerized accounting systems. A cash management system offers the following benefits:

Provides information to evaluate the impact of purchasing decisions before expenditures are committed.

Facilitates raising additional funds which are projected to be needed in the future, providing sufficient time to obtain financial support.

Sharpens awareness of deadlines, particularly those for tax deposits and other periodic payments.

Provides checkpoints (planned controls) to compare against actual results. Significant deviations from expected results serve as a signal that programs are not moving along as planned. This could mean that plans are not realistic and may need revision.

Predicts when and in what quantity the dollars will be coming into and out of the business. The cash flow forecast is a tabulation of company plans expressed in terms of their impact on incoming and outgoing dollar flow.

Establish Collegial Relationships and Exchanges of Information among Peers

Entrepreneurial owners and managers have few places to look internally to find the empowering stimulation they require in order to keep growing their business. They usually cannot turn to their employees or secretaries for such understanding conversations. Hence, it is important for an owner, founder, chief visionary, leader, or company executive to maintain a cutting-edge mentality by having frequent conversations with people like him at collegial gatherings such as chamber of commerce meetings and association conventions. Exchanges of information among peers help them renew their pledge to be owner-leaders, and not just highly compensated employees of their own companies.

Assure That Education for Managers and Employees Is Practical and Focused

Closely related to the point of collegial relationships mentioned in the previous section is practical education for both the managing executives of a company and its employees. I say practical because a lot of what passes for business education nowadays is not only worthless, it's potentially destructive.

Case in point. An automotive supplier in the Midwest subjected its first-line supervisors to a week of soft[3] training aimed at improving their skills in handling workers. One of the attendees was Bob, a twenty-year employee of the company, the last fifteen years as first-line supervisor. Bob was one of the old timers, a gruff but respected supervisor who took no shit from any of his workers but knew how to get the work out.

During the training period the instructor persuaded Bob to smile when talking with his workers and to speak in dulcet tones. Bob grumbled about this, but being the trooper that he is, agreed to give it a try.

The Monday following the week of training, Bob greeted his workers at the start of his shift with a smile and pat on the back. Needless to say, the workers were shocked. This wasn't the same snarling boss they knew and feared; this was some kind of alien who had taken over Bob's body. They didn't know how to respond. Instead of creating good will, the training Bob received caused a slowdown in Bob's department as workers struggled to figure out what was going on with Bob; they weren't accustomed to responding to kindness. It took about two weeks before Bob's supervisor, the department manager, stepped in and stopped the charade. Bob soon returned to his old snarling self and production soon moved back to its former levels.

---

[3] Soft training refers to intangible subjects such as improving your skills in working with others. By contrast, hard training refers to learning a specific technique such as statistical process control, shipping methods, machine set-up, and productivity systems.

There's been a lot of this sow's ear into a silk purse type of management education over the years. If that wasn't bad enough, it's been well complemented (and complicated) by management fads such as matrix management, theory Z, one minute management, management by walking around, and a host of other fads stretching back to post World War Two.

But practical education—the kind that improves employees' performance such as quality control techniques and reengineering principles—enhance the value of employees and contribute to company performance.

Continually Improve Product and Service Value and Reduce Waste

It's incumbent upon every company executive to find ways to continually improve the value of company products and services. Look at it this way: Every year the prices of the parts and materials and services you purchase for your business rise. Sure, there are exceptions, but on the whole, you can expect upwards price pressure. And the demands of customers increase. What served their needs in past years no longer suffice. They insist on better quality, improved customer service, and lower prices. The company owner is caught in this unyielding squeeze.

Reducing waste is an essential component part of this process, particularly in manufacturing operations where the generation of scrap and rework can assume proportions high enough to drown the company in red ink. And scrap and rework is a sure sign that quality is slipping, and your customers will not tolerate poor quality products and services for long. Competitors are always anxious to snatch your customers at the first sign of weakness on your part.

In such an environment companies have no choice—assuming they want to survive and prosper—but to increase the value of their product and service offering.

Do Not Micro Manage

I manager I know burned out and was forced to take a medical leave because he didn't know how to delegate. Every employee from supervisor to CEO who supervises the work of others cannot afford the luxury of following up every detail. It's not only impossible, it's damaging to the morale of subordinates whom you have charged with the responsibility of fulfilling their duties. Getting too involved borders on micro-managing the business. This negates the trust delegated to others to achieve results, and stunts the growth of the business. Again, the leader's emphasis has to be on the need to *lead*, not *do*.

It's almost an inescapable conclusion that companies with micro-managing executives do not perform as well in the marketplace. Their sales and profits are invariably lower than they should be.

Maintain Compliance to Regulatory Requirements

Businesspeople have watched passively as government agencies have taken control of just about every facet of corporate behavior from safety requirements to the number of hours a truck driver can steer his truck down the road. Not to mention the overwhelming tax documents needed for compliance. Business owners are stuck with regulations on products and services and therefore it is important that they know which rules apply to their businesses.

And it's not getting any better. Today governmental regulations are choking companies, especially small to midsized companies, where red tape costs have run amok along with their restrictive chokehold on business activity.

In such an environment, pity the deluged business owner or manager who somehow overlooks a minor detail and is cited by the government (city, county, state, or feds) for non-compliance. Wrangling your way out of such a tangled mess is expensive and time consuming.

Unfortunately, there is no easy answer to this predicament other to take steps to assure fulfillment of every requirement. Failure to do so can result in severe fines and even shutting down your business.

<u>McCain's Maxim #3:</u> Your first obligation as the guiding executive of your company is to determine what tasks are ground floor requirements. Some are more important than others are, and it's up to you to determine their order. There is no cookbook formula to assist you. Every company is different. The tasks described above may or may not fit your circumstances, and you may need others as well.

CHAPTER THREE

Articulate the Company's Mission Statement

It Keeps Owners and Managers
Focused on the Company's Purpose

As a company grows, owners and managers can get too involved in day-to-day minutia and lose the entrepreneurial spirit. There is a way to keep the company's eyes focused on its purpose. It's called the mission statement. Articulating the company's mission keeps all managerial eyes focused on the job ahead. This chapter shows how to construct a mission statement based on the purpose and objectives of the business. It's the foundation on which the company builds its policies and procedures. All financial and operating plans flow from the company's mission. Without exception, the personality or culture of the company will mimic the personality of the owners or leaders.

Here's the underpinning statement: Behave the way you want your company to behave. Always recognize that, without exception, the personality or culture of the company will mimic the personality of the owners or leaders. Behave the way you want your company to behave.

The procedure described below explains the method of formulating a simplified corporate mission statement to be used as a communication device with customers, employees, and the public.

The Mission Statement Explained

A mission statement communicates to employees and management the company's overall expectations, direction, and focus. All goals, policies, and procedures are developed within the parameters set forth in the mission statement. *The basic function of a mission statement is to convey to customers, employees, and the public the purpose for the company's existence.*

The goals of the company begin with the mission statement. Short and long range plans are formulated from this statement. Descending goals are then developed for each major function within the company. This process continues throughout the entire organization. Objectives or action plans are the timetables added to the goals to perpetuate and measure the process throughout the company.

The mission statement is a description of the company leadership's vision and direction, written in terms easily understood by all employees. The company leadership's vision is the way the company plans to conduct business. Management and employee decisions are not to override the mission statement, which is the basic premise of why they are in business. The mission statement's purpose is to provide a companywide bond and a single-minded approach to generating profits.

In format, the mission statement is a short declaration describing the company's relationship and expectations with respect to customers, employees, and the public. The most obvious is profit (remember: in business, profit is not a dirty word); but there may be other reasons for the company's existence, *provided it is profitable.* Other reasons may be a provider of necessary services to the people in the community and an opportunity for personal growth and development of the company's employees.

The mission statement lists critical attributes necessary to instill the values of the company in employees. Key words are used, such as quality, customer service, and teamwork. The purpose is to set a common direction for everyone within the company.

It may also describe what the company provides for its employees. This is a realistic and truthful statement of management's concern for the safety, well being, and contentment of its employees.

The entire mission statement may be three sentences or three paragraphs, but should be confined to one page. It must be easily understood and brief. If employees do not understand what it means, they will not respond as intended. If the mission statement is too long, employees will not remember its contents. (This runs contrary to what many companies publish. Some mission statements run into literally pages.)

One of the best mission statements I have ever read belongs to S. C. Johnson for its product Raid: *Raid Kills Bugs Dead!* You will find this listed, along with many others in this book's appendix. It contains a comprehensive list of typical mission statements from mostly well-known companies to help stimulate your thinking.

Once you have drafted and approved the mission statement, post it in a conspicuous place in the company. All employees should sign the mission statement, to demonstrate everyone's commitment to the company's purpose. The mission statement then becomes the basis for decision making and performance evaluations.

Company leaders are keepers of the vision and the designers of the mission statement. Other managers may be involved in the statement formulation, but the responsibility of the completed mission statement remains with the president and vice-president as well as company owners.

Another way of expressing that same thought is that good leaders do the right thing and good managers do things right. In a small to midsized business, you have to be both. Don't let ownership cloud your leadership.

Questions to Ask before Formulating a Mission Statement
1. What type of business do you have?
2. What is the purpose of this business?
3. What is the key message or phrase to describe your business in one sentence?

4. What is your reason for starting your own business?
5. What is your product or service?
6. Can you list three unique benefits of your product?
7. List the top three objections to buying your product/service immediately?
8. Who is your target market?
9. Who is your competition?
10. What is the pricing of your product versus competition?
11. Are you making any special offers?
12. What plans do you have for advertising & promotions?
13. How will you finance company growth?
14. Do you have the management team needed to achieve your goals?
15. What is your vision for the company? To help you with this task, complete the form shown on the following page.

Discover Important Information You Want Included in Your Mission Statement

Start by listing the factors that will go into your mission statement in the left hand column titled *Factors*. In the next column rate its importance. "A" means of great importance, "B" means of medium importance, "C" means of little importance. Finally, in the column to your right, describe what your vision for each factor is.

Factors	Importance	How Do You See the Company?
Profit		
Market Type		
Market Niche		
Sales Growth		
Company Growth		
Competition		
Creativity		
Training		

Quality		
Customer Service		
Technology		
Safety		
Ethics		
Vendors		
Community		
Others:		

McCain's Maxim #4: The mission statement is a process of discovery. Draft a compelling mission statement that is as brief as possible but contains the image you want to impart to your employees, customers, and community. Use the form above and ask yourself the key fifteen questions contained in the section immediately before the form. This process will help you evolve a mission statement that will identify the core values of your company. To guide your efforts make your mission statement SMART: (specific, measureable, achievable, relevant, and timely).

CHAPTER FOUR

Develop an Organizational Structure
to Match the Mission Statement

The Right Organizational Structure
Keeps the Company on Track

Organizational structure flows from the mission statement, but some inexperienced owners and managers insist on creating organizational structures that are totally inappropriate for their companies.

Case in point. Jerry, a laid-off middle manager from a large lamp manufacturer in New Jersey borrowed venture capital and bought a bankrupt zinc die cast lamp manufacturing company, landed a large order with three major department stores, and was off and running.

Two years later, with orders still pouring in, he faced insolvency. When he called Mark, a long time friend and consultant, to analyze his problems, it didn't take too long to discover one of the root causes of the problem. Jerry and Mark had the following conversation in Jerry's office:

Mark said, "I think I found what the problem is, Jerry. At least the main one."

"Go ahead, let me know. Give it to me straight. We've worked together many times before, Mark. You know I can handle the truth."

"Okay, as long as you put it that way, I'll skip the ego-salving introduction and put it bluntly. You've got too many employees working for you."

Mark's face dropped about a foot. "What? I don't get it."

"Maybe I didn't express that exactly right. What I meant to say is that you've got too many staff and overhead functions for a company your size. Many of those functions don't need to be there, at least not as full-fledged departments. Not for a small company like yours."

Mark shook his head. "You're losing me, Mark. Too many functions? I don't get it."

Mark sighed. As a consultant he had run across similar situations many times before. "Okay, look at the production planning process. You've got separate departments for inventory control, scheduling, shipping and traffic."

"Hey, come on Mark. Every manufacturer needs those departments."

"They need those functions, not those departments. There's a difference."

"Not much of a difference," Jerry grumbled.

"Oh, yeah? Each of those departments has a manager, a secretary, three or four supervisors, and half-dozen clerks. You're behaving as if you're General Motors or Microsoft. The giant companies need large staffs because they have billions of dollars in sales. Your sales last year was fifteen million."

"I guess it kind of slipped by me. I get so damned involved with running this place every day that I'm probably forgetting the big picture."

"Probably?" Mark snorted. "Listen, buddy, you're up to your nose in water and drowning. Your organization chart, the one you so proudly display over the desk in your office, looks like you copied it from IBM."

"But we do need the functions you mentioned, and in fact we need every one of the functions I've displayed on the organization chart."

"Sure do, but you don't need entire departments. Lots of the functions can be handled by employees wearing many hats."

"I see your point," Jerry said.

"The problem is once you create a department, then you need a manager, and the manager needs a secretary and

supervisors, and they all need office space and desks, and before you know it, you've created a bureaucracy that rivals the federal government. The difference is you need to make a profit. All the fed has to do is print more money."

Jerry sighs. "You're right, Mark. Let's start chopping."

"We will, Jerry, but let's first go back to your company's mission statement. Quoting it, 'to sell the highest quality lamp at the lowest price to discriminating buyers.' Start with that, then construct a new organization structure to fit the needs of the company."

"Okay, Mark, you've got a deal. You've opened my eyes. I won't make the same mistake, again"

The point is that without a clear mission statement and the organizational structure to support it, mistakes as Jerry made are all too common. Here's how to keep on track:

List of Functions for the Organizational Structure
Probably the first task after completing the mission statement is to develop a list of functions for every area of the company. The list shown below is an example. It may or may not include all of the functions of your company, so use it as a guide *only* as you develop your own.

General Management Function
Reporting Relationships
Reports to Owners
Administrative, Financial, Operational, Sales & Marketing

Measurements of Performance
Profitability
Facilities and Equipment Preservation
Low Record of Litigation and Unresolved Customer Complaints
Budgeting Process on Time with Quarterly and Annual Budgets
    within Determined Variance Levels
Completed Performance Evaluations for employees

Companywide safety record shows no preventable accidents.

General Responsibilities
Administrative Policies
Capital Budgeting, Approval, & Expenditure
Compensation Policy
Employee Development
Execution of Contracts
Strategic Planning
Organizational Development
Operating Policies
Employees Policies
Public Relations
Quality Control Standards
Financial & Advisory Relationships
Fiscal Policy
Expense Budget Approval
Tax, Legal & Insurance Approval
Budget Process, Formation & Analyzing
Administer Professional Services
Pricing Policy
Profit Goal Attainment
Market Share and Market Evaluation
Customer Relations
Profit & Expenses
Revenue & Sales Volume
Capital Improvement & Expenditures

Administration Function
Reporting Relationships
Reports to General management function
Payroll, Employees, Accounts Payable and Receivable,
        Receptionist, and Secretaries report to the
Administrative function.

Measurements of Performance

Maintain and Monitor Cash Flow within Tolerances and Pre-
determined Acceptance Limits
Completed Annual Performance Evaluations
All Reporting on Time
Information to Accountant on Time
Assure that there is no form of discrimination anywhere in the
company regarding, sex, race, creed, age, or religion
All shipping orders received from shipping are billed

General Responsibilities
Develop and Administer Computer Hardware Systems for
company
Develop Reporting Systems
Systems Backups and Develop Archives and Storage
Develop Historical Systems for Variance Reporting
Management Information System
Train back-up for your position
Manage Accounting Process
Perform Internal Audits
Liaise with Financial and Accounting Sources
Budget Preparation and Monitoring for Departments
Cash Flow Forecasting and management of company Cash
Credit Verification, management and Collections
Preparation of Operating Reports and Cost Controls
Payroll with Departmental Labor Breakdowns
Establish Cut off Times for Reports
Overhead Preparation, Calculation and Allocation
Tax Preparation
Profitability Summary
Weekly management and Current Position Report
Employees Evaluations
Communication between Departments
Enforce Adherence to Policies
Work area is clean and maintained.

Sales & Marketing Function

Reporting Relationships
Reports to General management function

Measurements of Performance
Sales Volume, Customer Satisfaction, Customer Retention
Ratio, Gross Profit, Selling Cost Percent, Market Penetration,
Number of New Customers
Labor Budget Adherence.
Assure that there is no form of discrimination anywhere in the
       company regarding, sex, race, creed, age, or religion

General Responsibilities
Hire, Train, Supervise, and Evaluate Sales People
Monitor Inventory Availability
Maintain Price Lists and Records
Telemarketing and Solicitation
Analyze and Improve Marketing Systems
Coordinate Paper Flow and Internal Communications
Enforce Policies, Procedures, Cost Controls, and Budgeting
Marketing Plans, Strategy, Analysis and Advertising
Budget Preparation and Sales Achievement
Establishing Sales and Marketing Quotas
Customer Relations, Sales Analysis and Review
Department Cost Controls
Employee Productivity
Employee Training
Work area is clean and maintained
Maintain printed material inventory
Develop printed material (such as catalogs, price sheets.)
Demographic Evaluations & New Market Potential
Build Strong and Loyal Customer Base
Service Customers by Quotes, Anticipating Needs, Resolving
       Concerns and Complaints, and Providing Technical
       Support
Develop and Implement Marketing and Promotions

F

Assist with Collections
Recommend Additions and Deletions to product lines
Adhere to Credit Policy and Procedures
Forecast Sales, Review Financial Results and Reports, and
Maintain Records

Operations Function
Reporting Relationships
Reports to General management function

Measurements of Performance
Labor Budget Adherence Satisfaction
Customer Satisfaction
Shipping Time and Accuracy at or Below Estimates
Safety Record Shows No Preventable Accidents
Inventory control at maximum level for minimum cost
Assure that there is no form of discrimination anywhere in the
company regarding, sex, race, creed age, or religion.

General Responsibilities
Supervise shop employees, including On-Site Training,
Scheduling, Establishing Goals, meeting unit Standards, and
Employee Evaluations
Coordinate Daily Work Flow
Service Customers
Process Orders for Delivery
Train back-up for your position
Work area is clean and maintained
Process Customer Returns for Credit or Repair, Matching
Returns to Purchase Orders, Assessing Condition of Inventory,
Coordinating Warranties
Manage Inventory Including Arranging Storage, Supervising
Security, and Controlling Shrinkage
Manage Equipment Including Coordinating Repairs,
Maintenance and Licensing
Maintain Yard, Building, and Supplies

Administer Safety Program for all employees
Coordinate Paper Flow, Maintain Records, and Analyze and
     Improve Systems
Enforce Policies and Procedures
Schedule Work Flow for Shop
Coordinate Repair and Maintenance of Company Equipment
Implement and Supervise Requisition System
Track Productivity for Labor and Material Cost
Supervise Weekly Work Assignments
Employee Performance and Evaluation Procedures
Discipline

Purchasing Function
Reporting Relationships
Reports to Operations function

Measurements of Performance
Inventory Turns
Product Quality
Vendor Discount Level
Back Order Ratio
Shipment Errors at or Below Minimum Set
Product Cost to Term Cost Ratio
Assure that there is no form of discrimination anywhere in the
     company regarding, sex, race, creed, age, or religion.

Specific Responsibilities
Monitor Stock Status
Purchase Product
Adhere to Inventory Budget
Control Purchase Orders
Control Product Quality
Control Receipt Date
Coordinate Delivery
Coordinate Special Orders
Negotiate for Most Favorable Terms and Price

Develop and Administer Vendor Agreements
Coordinate Returns and Credits
Plan Inventory and Equipment Flow
Forecast Cash Requirements
Assist with Physical Counts and Checks
Reconcile Inventory Counts

General Responsibilities
Maintain Price List and Assist Sales for Updates
Liaise with Sales, other Operations, and Accounting
Maintain Records
Develop Purchasing Procedures
Train a back-up for your position
Work area is clean and maintained
Adhere to Company Policies and Procedures
Inventory Control
Materials Cost Control for Company
Vendor Relations

Safety and Quality Assurance Function
Reporting Relationships
Reports to the General Manager

Measurements of Performance
No accidents or serious injuries
Company complies with all applicable federal and state safety,
        environmental, and industrial regulations
Safety Training and Awareness
Become Certified Professional
Conduct Safety and Quality Audits

General Responsibilities
Develop and maintain company safety and quality assurance
        manuals
Prepare capital budget requests as appropriate for the function
Interpret safety rules in the employee handbook

Develop and implement disaster preparedness procedures
Assure that safety manuals are available and used on the jobs
    when appropriate
Instill the Total Quality management (TQM) philosophy and
    techniques in the company
Conduct TQM and Safety workshops for company employees
Maintain safety records as required by federal and state laws
Train backups

Position Titles and Organizational Structure
        The next task involves defining position titles and the
accompanying organizational structure. In corporate
organizations, each salaried or non-exempt salaried position
usually has a title. The title often implies the level of
responsibility and authority of that position in the company.
Although the actual level of responsibility and authority may
not exist for the position, perception often becomes the reality
when dealing with customers, vendors, employees from other
departments or divisions, and other business contacts.
Therefore, it is important that position titles be consistent
between departments and divisions of all companies, especially
in midsized companies.

Position Titles
        Definitions of the positions may vary from company to
company, but the titles described below are universal.

President- The most senior corporate operating executive of the
company. This position reports to the corporation's board of
directors as represented by the chairman of the board.

Executive Vice-President - This is a corporate officer with the
responsibilities and authority delegated to this corporate level
by the board of directors. Use of the term executive indicates a
position of greater responsibility and authority than a vice-
president. It is a means of establishing different rungs on the

hierarchical ladder in the corporate office. This position often has profit and loss (P & L) responsibility with several P & L centers reporting to the position in large companies. In smaller firms, the position may denote P & L responsibility of the largest profit center or the one most critical to the success of the business.

Vice-President - This is a corporate officer with the responsibilities and authority delegated to this corporate level by the board of directors. This position often has P & L responsibility, but many corporations will use the title for staff functions such as, finance, human resources, and research and development (R&D).

General Manager - This title is used for non-corporate officer positions with responsibility and authority for multiple functions and profit and loss of the business segment. Occasionally, the title will be used for a position with multi-functional reporting relationships, but without any P & L responsibility.

Manager - Salaried professional employees report to the position. Oftentimes this title is used for staff positions reporting to general management or corporate officer positions. On these occasions, the positions have significant responsibilities and authority. The manager title always implies budget responsibility although, in some cases, it is not practical to have a separate budget for the position.

Supervisor - This title is used for positions to which hourly and non-exempt salaried employees report. The title implies supervisory responsibility of people, and does not include financial forecasting, expense monitoring and control, and employee pay rate control. Although every company may define supervisors differently, usually the term is used for the first line or front line of management.

Consultant - This title is often used in a corporate structure to identify a very experienced individual with special knowledge of the product, process, or business and its unique operating environment. Usually this position does not have any direct reporting employees. This position will often report to the businesses senior operating manager or corporate officer.

Specialist - This title is used for professional salaried employees with specialized knowledge in their field. For example, engineering, production planning, inventory control, accounts payable, payroll, human resource recruiters. These are all examples of professional areas in which a specialist position may be employed. The specialist is often the most senior and experienced employee in the department. On many occasions, the specialist will be an individual who can guide and teach other employees how to perform their respective jobs in his or her specific professional area. Specialists are usually considered the top grade individual contributor in their respective organizations and do not have any responsibility for managing or supervising employees because they may not have the interpersonal skills or desire to become successful supervisors or managers. The title of specialist can be used at all levels of the organization and does not reflect the salary earning capability of the position. Specialists reporting to higher level managers or operating executives usually have salaries corresponding to their reporting level.

Administrator - This title is used for either exempt or non-exempt salaried positions with an administrative support role in a department. The support is often provided in data entry, record maintenance, scheduling or the assignment of clerical tasks. This term is preferred over the use of assistant which implies a gofer instead of a position with defined responsibilities and authority.

Clerk - This title is usually reserved for non-exempt salaried and hourly positions throughout an organization. The job requirements are defined by job descriptions which clearly define the work elements to be accomplished in the position. Overtime pay is required by law for anyone working more than eight (8) hours/day and forty (40) hours/week in a clerical position in an office, manufacturing, or warehouse area.

Organizational Structure

Large organizations often divide themselves into smaller, decentralized units in order to improve management and control of the entity. When this is done, naming the individual units often becomes a challenge because the organizational terms will imply a certain size or position in the organization. Here are the common organizational structures:

Division - A separate P&L center with a corporate officer or general manager as the executive responsible for its performance.

Operation -A separate business unit that is multi-functional but without P&L responsibility.

Function - A function is a specific discipline, such as finance, information systems, production, engineering, marketing, sales, that is an integral component of a division or operation.

Department - A group of positions under a manager or supervisor. Several similar departments may be combined into a function.

Summary of Core Tasks

Review the financial processes, operating systems, and organizational layouts of the company, and with management's involvement, construct a functional organization chart.

Redistribute tasks as appropriate. Often the task of constructing an organization chart exposes weaknesses.

Create a positional organization chart and assist in the assigning of employees to key positions.

Introduce the positional organization chart to the company's employees and customize as needed.

Review and revise job descriptions for key employees, outlining:
A) Basic functions
B) Reporting relationships
C) Responsibility and authority
D) Principal duties
E) Measures of performance

McCain's Maxim #5: Creating and maintaining a functional organizational structure is key to the company's ability to operate successfully. Every employee in the company should have the opportunity to contribute his or her piece about their roles and reporting relationships. It's important to have everybody buy into how the company functions or intends to function. Review the mission statement and organizational structure every five years or so.

CHAPTER FIVE

Construct a Business Plan

The Business Plan Is the Company's Roadmap

There is nothing more fundamental to the success of a company than constructing a business plan. It sets the stage for the company's growth and success.

Unfortunately, many business owners and managers don't take the time to make plans, and consider the business plan just another piece of paper to clutter their desks. Greg, a consulting associate of mine told me about Stan, one of his clients, a plumber who decided to take the plunge (pardon the pun). He borrowed money from a rich uncle to buy a plumbing supply manufacturing company. Somewhere along the line Greg and his client had this conversation. I am reporting it here as best as I can recollect:

"Stan, I'm thinking now may be as good a time as any to write a business plan for your company. What do you think?"

"The business is doing pretty good. Why do I need a plan? What's it going to get me besides another bunch of useless papers I'll file away and never look at again?"

"If you had borrowed capital from a venture capital firm or a bank you would have been required to write a business plan before you got the first penny."

"But I didn't. Uncle Sydney came through. So why do I need one now?"

"It's a blueprint for your company's future. It lets you know where you're going and if you're on track to get there. Look at it this way. You get in your car and drive to Louisville. That's three hundred miles away. You have to be there at 4:00pm for a business meeting with one of your key customers. How do you know when you have to leave the house?"

Stan smiled. "Hell, that's easy. Driving to Louisville takes me oh, about four hours."

"Four hours? You've got to be kidding. If you do it in four hours you've got to average . . ." Greg takes out his pocket calculator. "That's 75 miles per hour. Ten miles per hour over the speed limit. And you're on state roads. State troopers will bag you."

Stan shrugs. "Look, I've done it before . . . once . . . and never got a ticket."

"Okay, you did it once. You were lucky. Bet you a steak dinner that if you do it again, your chances of getting away with that kind of speeding is going to land you a hefty fine."

Stan hesitates. "Come to think of it, I remember catching a state cop behind a hedge clocking speeders going in the other direction."

"The point is it could have happened to you. Anything can happen that causes you to lose time. You could have had a flat or run out of gas, for example. You would have missed that important meeting. But if you had a plan—how many miles you needed to go every hour, and if you checked your mileage after every hour—if you had that flat tire you could have made the time up and made that meeting on time. Only because you would have been conscious of what mileage you needed to accomplish."

"I see what you mean, Greg."

"The same principle holds true for a business plan with a timetable and list of events to make your plan happen. It makes sure your company is positioned for the future, and it provides you an opportunity to check progress along the way and take corrective action if you stray from plan."

"In other words, it keeps my company on schedule."

"You got it, buddy."

Do You Know Where You Are Going?

As Yogi Berra once said, "You've got to be very careful if you don't know where you're going, because you might not get there."

A successful business plan is one that focuses your thinking, helps you establish a realistic business strategy, improves your operations, and wins for your company the financing and other support it needs.

Written business plans, broadly speaking, are usually put together for either of two purposes: to prepare for a significant event, such as obtaining financing, or to guide the company's operations for a particular period, usually a year.

Keep in mind, in writing the plan you'll invariably take two steps forward and one step back. It's an uneven path, fraught with unforeseen frustrations and difficulties. Thrashing out those difficulties is a key part of the planning process.

Being in business is a journey, not a destination—with *no* paved roads or freeways (despite what some franchisers would have you believe). Every business travels into the uncharted territory of the future. But, no matter how good a driver you may be, how well you know the route, or how quickly you can load and unload the vehicle, if you fail to put fuel in the tank, air in the tires, oil in the engine, water in the radiator, or otherwise adequately maintain and service the vehicle, it will soon grind to a halt. You'll go nowhere.

Sadly, this is the case with most small business or midsized owners and managers. They're good drivers -- plumbers, hairdressers, retailers, lawyers, accountants, printers or whatever their trade or profession may be—but they oftentimes haven't a clue what's required to maintain and manage their companies. So they rarely make it to their chosen destinations. To complete the journey to your chosen destination you need a suitable business vehicle.

Who needs a plan? Anyone who starts or runs a business needs a plan. It's as simple as that . . . no ifs, ands, or buts. Don't think that you or your business is any different. Successful companies all have plans … unsuccessful companies don't.

Why do *you* need a business plan? The main reason is *you*! A good business plan will help *you*. Writing a business plan is not as difficult or daunting as *you* might think and even if it were... it is something *you* must do anyway!

There are a few things that you can do right now to get started:

Think about the background and history of your company. Write a general description of your business, how long you have been in operation, and some basic financial details.

Write a few paragraphs about the nature of the products or services you offer. Use language that a non-expert will understand. What do you sell? How is the product used? What need does it serve?

Think about your competitive position in the market. Write out answers to these few basic questions: What are the advantages of your product (cheaper, better quality, unique features, and so forth)? Are there any disadvantages? (Be honest!) Who is your competition? Describe their products, advantages, and problems.

Next think about your customers. Write a description of some typical customers. Who are they? Where are they? Why do they buy? When do they buy? Who makes the decision to buy?

Write a clear statement of your business objectives. What are your goals in terms of sales, profits, traffic to your website, and other measures you consider significant. Set some objectives for three months, six months, one year, and two years. Start by thinking about your one-year goals, and then work backwards to formulate the benchmarks you need to reach at six months, and then three months from now.

These are just a few of the considerations that need to go into a powerful business plan, but even these few points will get you started. Spend some time on your business plan; you owe it to yourself and your business.

Business Plan Analysis

Business planning is the science of planning large scale operations, specifically of manoeuvring forces into the most advantageous positions prior to taking action. It is important when considering this procedure that your thinking adheres closely to this definition of strategy because it will help you to specifically define your business activities and your future direction.

Careful design of a business plan will allow you to respond appropriately to business conditions and opportunities, to meet specific objectives, and to avoid many unpleasant surprises down the road. Business planning makes the difference between mediocrity and superiority. That is why you are here—isn't it?

The business planning cycle is constant, whether the plan is being designed to affect the entire business operation or to assist in making a single decision affecting only one part of the business.

Stages in the business planning cycle are:

Review the current situation

Establish the objective

Define the factors which will affect the plan

Establish the strategies needed to reach the objective (develop the *business action plan*)

Review your strategies

Implement the business action plan (BAP)

Review progress periodically and, if necessary, modify the objective, the BAP or both to reflect new conditions.

The next step is to establish the current condition of the organization. Take a present day snapshot. Briefly, take stock of your present situation regarding all areas of operation. Be brief; one page should be all you need. Here are factors to evaluate:

Market environment

Products and services

Pricing and profitability

Customers

Distribution

Administration and management

Financial resources.

     The objectives should be:
Appropriate. They should ring true for what you expect to be doing.

Acceptable. They should fall within industry and political environments.

Feasible. They should permit appropriate and timely response to contingencies.

Measurable Over Time. They should be able to be monitored and controlled over time periods extending perhaps over a number of years.

Motivational. They should be aggressive yet achievable.

Understandable. They should make sense to others not familiar with your concepts.

Try to assure that objectives are zero-based, not extrapolated from past trends or current budgets. Point them to the future without reference to past or present conditions. And make your objectives read as a simple *statement of intent*. For example:

To increase customer base by 15 percent during 2012

To establish a maintenance service contract program by 2012.

To train and develop Mr. Jones as a programmer in 2012.

To achieve a 10 percent increase in Western sales by 2013.

Your objectives can be as wide or as narrow in scope as you want them to be. Regardless, the business planning process *does not change.*

The next step is to assess the factors most likely to change your business plan. Factors likely to affect your planning can include virtually anything: the weather, political influences, environmental considerations, the economic climate, or simply time, among others.

It is important that you give full rein to your imagination at this stage. Think laterally and try to list all of the external factors (those which are not within your capacity to control) that may have an impact on your business or long term personal plans. What you are trying to do here is establish best case/worst case scenarios in order to eliminate, if possible, the potential to be surprised along the way to achieving your objectives.

Develop the Business Action Plan
    The business action plan must include:

A written statement of the objective.

A brief review of the current position.

A summary of factors affecting the plan.

A *detailed, written strategy* designed to achieve the objectives - a step-by-step how-to manual.

A record of who will be accountable for performing each step of the plan.

A schedule for implementation of the plan specifying check point dates or other monitoring devices.

A notation on the action to be taken, by whom, in the event that unforeseen circumstances interfere with the smooth implementation of the plan at any stage.

A summary of review procedures to be used and a definition of the parameters which will be applied to determine successful completion of the plan.

    The objective you have set will determine the scope of the business action plan. Planning can be made on a global scale for the entire business operation or on a micro scale addressing one single issue. A full business plan will likely address the following issues:

Management and staffing.

Product or service descriptions.

Market analysis.

Market strategies.

Financial projections including a 12 month flexible budget schedule, a three year income projection, cash flow projections, pro forma balance sheets, a break even analysis, sources and uses of funds statements, capital expenditure budgets, financing requirements analysis, and investment decisions and schedules.

The lists described above are to be used as guidelines only. There may be any number of other issues or topics that you will want to include in your planning. Consideration must be given to all factors pertinent to your objectives.

Make each strategy a statement of imperative action. The strategy statement should serve to both impel action by those who will be implementing the strategy and to motivate them to see that the strategy succeeds.

Hint: Start each strategy with an action verb. Make each positive and not negative in context.

Before your BAP is implemented, it will be necessary to review the strategies you have designed to assure their validity. Use the *Business Review Checklist* (shown at the end of this section) as a guide to the conduct of this review process. It contains some, but probably not all, of the review criteria which you may want to apply. If your BAP fails this review you will need to re-think elements of the plan itself or perhaps even redefine the original objective, then repeat this review process.

Finally, take the necessary action to put your BAP into effect. Do this step by step according to defined schedules and monitoring check points that you have established for your plan.

Remember, this is a business plan and not a New Year's resolution. You will have spent considerable time, effort, and perhaps money, to design the plan so don't waste it by ignoring the end result and proceeding as if it didn't exist. *Your plan must be followed to be effective!*

Measure the degree of progress towards your objectives on a regular and continuing basis according to the review and monitoring criteria established. In some instances you will review your plan almost daily. In other cases you may want to review progress quarterly, semi-annually or even annually. The review periods will be determined by the nature of the plan, its criticality to operations, and its exposure to variable influences.

Progress reviews may be carried out in some cases by the planner alone. In others, a project review committee composed of all or some of the management team will be established and will hold regular, formal review meetings. Again, the nature and scope of the plan will determine this but whatever the circumstances, the *review must be carried out as specified in the Business Action Plan.*

The progress review may result in modifications to the original Business Action Plan. This is okay; remember that your plan should be flexible enough to respond to changing conditions. However, it is important to assure that any modifications to the BAP or to the original objectives be treated with the same methodical care as the original plan itself. Follow

all of the steps in the planning process when designing
modifications to the original Business Action Plan.

BUSINESS REVIEW CHECKLIST

Verify that all strategies define means to achieve the objective you set. If they merely restate the objective, modify or reject them.

Verify that your strategies are consistent with your analysis of the market place, your capabilities and your resources.

Assure that the return on investment is sufficient to justify the risks.

Assure that the strategies are consistent with the political environment within your company.

Assure that your strategies are based on facts and not on assumptions or a wish list.

Examine whether your strategies leave you critically vulnerable to sudden shifts in the market environment. Are all your eggs in one basket?

Examine your appraisal of the competition. Is it open-minded and honest?

Assure that your strategy is legal, that it doesn't violate the many federal, state, and local laws and ordinances.

Examine whether the success of your strategy is based on your ability window. What are the chances of failure? Do you need specialized assistance to succeed?

Assure that you have examined carefully all identifiable alternative strategies before accepting this one.

Verify that a sound deductive rationale exists for your business, strategy or recommendation.

Evaluation Criteria
The list below represents some, but not all, of the fact-finding consideration that should be included when analyzing and evaluating the present condition of the company, the setting of objectives and the design of strategies.

What business are we in?

What products or services do we currently offer?

What is our target market?

Why do our customers do business with us?

On a scale of one to 10, with 10 being the highest, how would our customers rate us? Why?

What is our market share?

Who is our competition? List the strengths and weaknesses of the top three.

What are our strengths:
    As I see them?

As our customers see them?
As our competitors see them?

What are our weaknesses:
   As I see them?
   As our customers see them?
   As our competitors see them?

What is our current organizational structure?

Did we grow in the past year? What factors contributed to the growth (or lack of growth)?

What portion of our business is produced by each product type or service?

What portion of our profit is produced by each product type or service?

Are all our products or services profitable? If not, why not?

Which expenses have increased as a percent of sales over the last three years?

Which expenses have decreased as a percent of sales over the last three years?

What portion of sales is produced each month for each product type or service?

At current levels of compensation and training, what is the capacity of the current staff?

What equipment do we have now?

What is the capacity of the equipment we have? Do we need more? Less?

What is the capacity of our current facilities?

What are the industry, technological, and environmental trends that are likely to affect us over the next:
   One year?
   Three years?
   Five years?

What Government regulations or restrictions will affect us in the next:
   One year?
   Three years?
   Five years?

What are the economic trends that will affect us in the next:
   One year?
   Three years?
   Five years?

What factors will aid our growth in the future?

What factors will limit our growth in future?

Where do we want to be in:
> One year?
> Three years?
> Five years?

Is there anything else we need to consider? Is there a personal agenda not contemplated in the questions we have asked so far?

Business Planning Synopsis

In developing the business plan process, don't forget to include the following steps:

Benchmark operating ratios so you know where you've been and where you want to go.

Locate your stage of the business life cycle stage (startup, survival, growth, or decline).

Identify the top challenges your company faces.

Identify the key performance indicators (KPI's) that you need to measure for company success. These may include:
1) Market-related issues
2) Financial planning and cost
3) Growth projections
4) Plant and facility plans
5) Cost objectives
6) Human resource development
7) R&D plans, projections, and projects

Also be sure to include the following information, because each of the items shown has a bearing on your business plans:
1) Projected sales and profits
2) Employee plans

3) Quality objectives
4) Customer satisfaction plans
5) Key internal quality and performance measures
6) Health, safety and environmental issues

And don't forget to document methods to track, update, revise and review progress to the BAP. Communicate the current state of the business plan to company employees. Keep them posted or their interest will flag.

McCain's Maxim #6: The business plan is the core document of your company. It identifies its vision, goals, and tells something about the competency of its guiding executives. This is not just another piece of paper: it is the soul of the company. Treat it as such.

CHAPTER SIX

Create a Financial Plan to Match the Business Plan

It's the Business Plan Reduced to Numbers

The company's financial plan is the numerical expression of the company's business plan, both short and longer term. This chapter shows how you do it.

The financial plan outlines the level of present financial requirements, objectives in terms of financial and performance ratios, pro-formas, current financing and financial requirements. Budgets are a required part of this plan along with variance analysis against actual. This section should be kept concise with supporting material (supplied to outsiders only when requested). In addition, the principal plan contains pro-forma financial forecasts. In carrying out your action plan for the coming year, these operating forecasts are your guide to business survival and profitability. This same information is utilized in the 12 month budget.

Before presenting your business plan to a lender or investor, review your financial statements with your CPA firm. This familiarity will increase your credibility and at the same time provide you with a good understanding of what the financial statements reveal about the viability of your business. Review with an outside source increases and hones presentation skills.

Financial Plan Format

Include the previous years' balance sheet and income statement. An additional two to three years provides information for trends. Some funding sources require a three year consistent profit history. Its components are:
Financial forecasts

Opening balance sheet (for new business divisions or acquisitions).

Projected income statement: This is a month-by-month pro-forma of projected income. It is prepared in conjunction with the 12 month budget prepared each year.

Budget: The budget is prepared month by month for each division and department based upon historical information and the forecast for the upcoming year.

Cash flow forecast (budget of cash in-flow and out-flow on a monthly basis for the next year of operation): The numbers from the projected income statement, budget and cash flow must all tie together.

Financing and capitalization.

Capitalization structure: Shows the current capitalization structure as well as the capitalization structure required to achieve an objective. Capitalization   should reflect a three year time horizon. This would also include funds required with loan or equity requirements. Before and after scenarios provide insight into the success mode of each operation. Equity offered or loans applied for would include the amount, terms, and when required.

Should a loan be required attach a detailed description of assets to be financed with cost quotations and appraisals.

Owners' equity (indicates owners' level of commitment to the program).

Equity or other offerings (includes the funding requirements, investor criteria, as well as the rationale).

EXAMPLE: Description

Building improvements	$ 3,000,000
Equipment & machinery	750,000
Vehicles	360,000
Non-recurring start-up	120,000
	$ 4,230,000

Financing:

Term loan requested	$ 1,000,000
Owners Equity	2,100,000
New Investor	2,130,000
	$ 4,230,000

Operating Loan

Line of credit applied for (new or increase, security offered)

Maximum operating cash requirement

Timing - refers to cash flow forecast

Present financing (if applicable)

Term loans outstanding: Balance owed, repayment terms, purpose, security held)

Current operating line of credit: Amount, security held

Operating Ratios
The important ratios that to be shown include the following:

Liquidity Ratios
Profitability Ratios
Current   Net Profit Margin
Quick Gross Profit Margin
Inventory/Working Capital
Cash Ratio
Return On Equity (ROE)
Return On Investment (ROI)
Earnings Per Share (EPS)
Productivity Of Assets
Activity Ratios (Annualized)
Leverage Ratios
Debt/Total Assets
Cash Flow/Liabilities
Long-term Debt/Equity
Current Liability/Equity
Acquisition Interest

Coverage
Receivable Turnover
Cash Turnover (days)

One of the best ways to measure how well the company is really doing is to compare pro-formas, budgets with actual performance ratios. Ratios also provide for a simple way to spot trends through graphs and charts.

Breakeven Analysis
Breakeven for a business, division or department is that point in sales volume where direct costs have been recovered, fixed expenses and overhead have been absorbed, and profits begin to accrue.

The importance of breakeven lies in the ability to know ahead of time the impact of financial decisions. Breakeven allows a decision maker to determine *what if* scenarios of hitting projections as well as not.

Financial Back-up Information
You need the following documents to support a position of growth, expansion, or financial support from outside sources:

Letters of intent. Without letters of intent, an acquisition's or new division's pro-formas are not supportable. Letters of intent might also include potential orders, customer commitments, and letters of support. Managers who want to break into new markets or other areas should gather these financial back-up documents:

A list of Inventory. Type of inventory, age, value, and method of valuation

A list of leasehold improvements

A list of leasehold improvements: description, when made

A list of fixed assets: description, age, and serial numbers

Price lists. This will support cost estimates

Description of insurance coverage

Insurance policies: amount of coverage, type of coverage.

Accounts receivable summary (Include aging schedule)

Accounts payable summary (Include schedule of payment)

Copies of legal agreements

Contracts, leases, franchise agreements, and mortgages

Appraisals of property and equipment

Financial statements for associated companies

Organizational structure for the financial area: Briefly describe who handles what within this department. How does information flow and how it is disseminated.

Financial performance

Emphasis on quality factors and management actions that lead to better market performance, market share gain, and customer retention.

Emphasis on improved productivity, asset utilization and lower overall operating costs.

Support for business strategy development and business decisions.

McCain's Maxim #7: A business plan without a financial plan is like an airplane flying without any instruments and the pilot blindfolded. It simply cannot perform its intended mission and will crash unexpectedly. Numbers speak eloquently of the company's success or failure to meet the goals of its business plan. The financial plan is the measure of how well your company is performing.

CHAPTER SEVEN
Finance Your Business

Proper Funding Gives the Company Life

The subtitle words *Proper Funding* says it all.
Nowadays many different avenues of financing a business are
springing up. Some of them are borderline illegal and others
plainly not in the interests of borrowers. Case in point:

Sam, with a background in selling automotive products,
wanted to start a new automotive supply store in a geographic
area that had no competitors. He cobbled together a business
and financing plan and tried to get capital the traditional ways:
by sinking his own money into the business and through money
from friends and relatives. But that wasn't near enough to
launch the business. He approached the banks, but in this tight
economy where banks are hoarding their capital he was turned
down. Next he tried venture capital firms, but his projected sales
volume was not enough to attract outside investors.

Then one day he came across an online ad advertising
the availability of loan capital. He eagerly filled out the
application online, providing confidential information about his
startup business and personal net worth and credit history.

After completing the form he waited for a response but
none was forthcoming. He tried calling the firm but found out
their phone had been disconnected. Uh oh! Bad sign.

Long story short. Sam discovered that the firm, a
shoestring operation bordering on a scam, had gone bankrupt.
Unfortunately, the bankrupt firm held all of Sam's confidential
information and who knows what they did with it? Shortly
afterward, Sam's identity was stolen and his efforts to open a
new store were stymied.

The bottom line is that financing your business requires careful planning, research and logistics. Identifying your capital needs and seeking the right and legitimate source of financing for filling those needs can get confusing and complicated at times. Even with pre-planning and diligent effort, the funding game can sometimes change in midstream, as economic climates shift causing the viability of various funding vehicles to vary over time.

You may have started in business as a specialist in a particular area of business-marketing, sales, R&D, or operations. Now as an owner or manager you need at least a general understanding of all aspects of business, especially appropriating and making efficient uses of funds.

The basis for your business may be a very sound concept, but funding new growth or maintaining existing growth can pose many challenges. Different types of capital requirements need different funding vehicles, all with different rules and steps similar in many ways to a game of monopoly or chess. Growing a business most often requires more capital than is readily available from existing cash flow or from the resources of the founder(s). Conversely, obtaining too much capital or raising it too soon can also cause other problems for the business.

The first step in this search is to learn and understand the pros and cons of the various types of capital needed by your enterprise. Capital comes into your business in two ways: as equity capital or as debt capital.

Equity financing is the investment of the owner(s) in the company. It stays in the company for the life of the business (unless replaced by other equity) and is repaid only when and if there is a surplus in the liquidation of the business-after all creditors are paid. Usually obtaining new equity is very difficult, especially during the early stages of the business.

Debt financing, on the other hand, can come into the business in a variety of ways. It comes for a defined period of time and is paid back with some form of interest.

The financing of your business can be further classified as start-up financing, which is usually equity, working capital financing, and growth financing. Start-up financing is the financing to get the company to an operational level including the costs of getting the first products or services to market. This is best done with equity and long term loans or leases.

Working capital is required to drive the day to day operations of the business. In most businesses the operational needs vary during the year (seasonality, inventory buildup, for example) and the working capital tides over the fluctuating expenses involved with doing the base business.

Growth capital is not tied to the yearly aspects of fueling the business. Rather, it is needed when the business is expanding or being changed in some significant and costly way that is expected to result in higher and increased cash flow. It is generally longer term than working capital and is paid back over a period of years from the profits of the business.

Knowing specifically what type of capital your business will need will put you in a stronger position when evaluating how and where to seek financing.

Narrowing the Search for Funds

Next you need to become familiar with the pros and cons of the various sources of financing and how each might cater to your specific capital needs. Are you an established business needing to buy fixed assets such as a new building or new equipment? Or do you need to add a new line of inventory to your stock? Are your needs for short-term money to help you through a seasonal cash crunch? If so, the typical source of financing for these kinds of needs is a traditional commercial bank.

If you are starting a new business and have sufficient collateral but need additional capital funds, the SBA loan program might be for you.

However, if your proposed business is on the leading edge of technology, and there is a potential for substantial growth, venture capital might be the appropriate financing source. These types of funding are discussed later in this chapter. Knowing the specific needs of your business will help to significantly narrow the scope of your funding search.

The methods for keeping abreast of funding options available to your business include networking with industry colleagues and successful business leaders in your region, soliciting the advice of financial experts, and reading of financial publications. Many entrepreneurs and investors are now also turning to on-line financing services, which are appearing with greater regularity. Some of these services attempt to match small businesses with investors, while others electronically post lists of companies seeking investors and then allow investors to examine the lists for companies of interest. Usually both the businesses and the investors pay fees to have access to this service.

These activities will help keep you positioned for the right funding move at the right time. Keep a sharp eye out for creative ways in which other successful businesses, similar to yours, are handling their funding. Follow up any leads for funding ideas that hold promise for your type of business. Most of all, don't get stuck in a rut of focusing on only one type of financing. Keep your options open. Hold several cards that can be played at the appropriate time for your business.

Yes, seek out and listen to the best advice you can find, but always closely check out the sources of potential funding. All financial sources seek, in various ways, return on investment in relation to the risk that they perceive they are taking. This is a given. Find out what they want in return, and when they want it. In addition, check out the people you will potentially be dealing with. Determine if they are reliable and if they know enough about your industry to be viable funding associates of your business.

Is the funder's style of business compatible with your vision and ethics? What kind of information about your business will they require to know? How far into your business will they pry? Your good questions will elicit appropriate funding information that will not only help your business' present situation, but also avoid funding scenarios that could severely handicap your business in the future.

What follows is a description of many of the options available for funding businesses in today's economy. The most commonly used funding sources are described for you more fully than the less used, narrower in scope methods.

Self Funding

The vast majority of businesses (close to 90 percent) are started with less than $100,000 and close to a third are begun with less than $10,000. This kind of money is usually available to the motivated entrepreneur by taking a close look at the personal resources at his or her disposal well in advance. Several of the most common self funding methods are described here.

The vast majority of new businesses are started with the main source of funding coming from personal savings or various forms of personal equity of the founders. This capital reflects the degree of motivation, commitment and belief of the founder in the enterprise. This type of investment also takes the shape of sweat equity, where individuals either donate their time or provide it at below market value to help the business get established. Many times entrepreneurs use profits from previous endeavors to pour into their new enterprise.

Many home-based businesses are begun while the founder is still working a regular job. The income from the job can both help support the owner during negative or low cash flow of the business set up phase and it can provide working capital to augment the business's cash flow. Usually when the business begins paying as well or better than the regular job, the entrepreneur can jump ship from his job and devote full time to building his new business.

Home equity loans may be the fastest growing method of raising money for individuals. Banks generally are willing to lend up to seven percent or more of a home's appraised value, minus any existing mortgages.

Home equity loans are generally offered through commercial banks or savings and loan associations. In some instances an approved home equity loan can be structured like a bank line of credit at slightly lower interest rates.

For tax purposes, you can deduct interest on up to $100,000 of debt on home equity loans, regardless of how you use the money. This makes a home equity loan attractive when looking for startup capital. Remember that since this money is secured by your home, the bank could foreclose if you fall behind in your payments.

Borrowing against your insurance policy is a personal type of loan that is becoming more available and more popular as a method for obtaining early financing for a small individually owned business. Other entrepreneurs have been known to completely cash in their life insurance policies. Many insurance companies have, in recent years, liberalized their criteria for allowing policy holders to borrow against the value of their policy.

Dipping into your tax-deferred retirement account can be a last resort for funding your business. This works best if you are more than 59 1/2 years of age. While the money in your Individual Retirement Account or 401(k) plan is technically available to you, you'll need to pay a 10 percent early withdrawal penalty plus regular income tax on money you withdraw. Obtaining funds with this method may still be worth it to you if no other financing avenues are available and you have the motivation.

It might be possible to get an unsecured loan on the strength of your retirement accounts. Although these accounts would not directly be pledged as collateral, the money could be withdrawn at a later date to repay the loan if it was required.

Pulling out the plastic for fast funding of your business is another avenue. MasterCard or Visa card holders with good credit now often receive credit limits of $10,000 and above. By being able to carry more than one credit card, as an entrepreneur you can considerably boost the total amount you can tap into at any one time.

Remember that obtaining funds through credit cards costs much more than bank loans. If you do use your credit cards for business funding, pay them off as quickly as you can. Paying only the minimum payments can extend interest for years without making much progress toward paying off the principal. Also, if your enterprise should not pan out, the credit card payments you will be stuck with may place you in a personal financial squeeze.

Often the best money to go after is the money that can be saved from the current costs and overhead of your ongoing business. This is a commonly overlooked source when business owners and managers are looking for the elusive pie-in-the-sky financing. A penny so saved is literally more than a penny earned on the bottom line, and a penny less borrowed. The interest is saved on the now lower loan amount and the time and expenses associated with finding additional financing.

The process of thoroughly searching through your operation for opportunities of savings and improved efficiencies will also allow you to learn more about the intricacies of your company, which will put you in a position to manage it better-a double return on your invested time and effort. The upshot is that by becoming more efficient and cost conscious, you will be in a stronger position at all times to qualify for refinancing options as they become needed and available.

Certain types of businesses can require an advance deposit from customers, which quickly spurs cash flow. If you can encourage cash payment instead of giving the customer credit, you avoid financing him. Similarly, you can also facilitate receiving cash quickly by granting cash discounts for early payments by customers. In any case, the more quickly your success has an impact on your suppliers and customers, the more likely they are to offer such deals.

If you have a yearlong customer, but your work peaks heavily in one season, you may want to offer your customer equalized billing all year round to help even out both your cash flow and their cash flow.

If you consistently work to build an excellent reputation in your field, you will find that your customers can work with you to help finance or partially finance your enterprise. Actively working with your suppliers or customers on an indirect form of loan called trade credit can help generate quick cash flow and also minimize expenses. This method can take a wide variety of forms. We will examine several of these methods here to give you possible alternatives that may be workable in your business.

Some suppliers, seeing an opportunity to grow themselves, may advance goods to you too, in effect, prime the pump if your venture looks particularly promising. You may have certain strength in being a debtor who pays back without abusing your creditors. As you generate the revenue from your sales you will have the funds to pay back the money owed and purchase additional goods. In a variation of obtaining goods advanced from suppliers, extended terms of 90 to 120 days or even longer can sometimes be pre-negotiated with suppliers during special circumstances or to assist with seasonal cash flow peaks and valleys.

If you use a manufacturer as part of your business, you may be able to utilize this manufacturer as an indirect investor, without having to borrow a penny. The manufacturer can lend you capital through use of their current raw materials, labor and technical know-how. They have wholesale leverage to assist or complete part of your design, set up, and assembly for far less than you would have to spend. Give them a good faith cash payment up front plus a small stake in your enterprise or a return on investment percentage based on the success of the finished product. The manufacturer, as a specialist, will be able to complete the job in less time than if you took on the whole job yourself. By both parties having a stake and motivation in the project, you may well be able to be successful without having to call in third-party investors, like bankers, venture capitalists or angels.

In certain situations, it may be beneficial for you to give a supplier, or even a property owner, equity for favorable long-term arrangements. This can free up some immediate cash to help grow your business.

You may be able to lessen your required cash outlay to suppliers by negotiating to obtain a cash discount for your early payment. As an example, two percent-10 means that a discount of two percent is granted if you pay for goods or services in full within 10 days.

For small businesses the variety of trade financing mentioned here are all usually easier to negotiate than is obtaining bank financing. One reason for this is the amount of cash as risk. If your supplier's variable costs represent 45 percent of the selling costs, then for $100,000 of financing the supplier has $45,000 cash as risk. The bank would have $100,000 cash at risk.

In any situation of this sort, creative ideas and clear communication and agreements can help you get over many funding humps in your business. You'll learn what trade credit opportunities like these are available with your suppliers and customers if you are willing to ask.

The need for capital can be lessened, especially in early stages of a business, through trading or bartering of your products or services with your suppliers. There are also associations that are formed to provide a network of barter opportunities among members.

This type of activity reduces needs for cash in the business. Caution should be taken to follow IRS regulations regarding this practice. Also, clear agreement is needed among the parties to assure proper value is granted for the traded goods.

Your employees can be your partners in solving needs for capital at your company in a variety of ways. You can offer certain senior and trusted employees to become common stockholders by investing in a purchase of your company stock. Employees usually have limited discretionary funds for stock purchases, but every dollar counts, and employee dollars usually come with the motivation to help improve the results of the company, thus the value of their investment. Common shareholders also have the right to have a say in the management of the company. Another possibility is to offer these employees nonvoting preferred shares of stock in return for their investment.

Many companies in their early phases of growth offer key employees or business partners' options to purchase certain amounts of stock at later dates, often at a discount price or on very generous terms. The stock options help supplement the employee's salary, which may be agreed to be below industry standards so that the company can retain this salary saving as capital for help in becoming successful.

By being part owners and participators in the profits, these desired employees will more likely choose to remain with your company instead of looking elsewhere for work. As with any individual investor, always document this investment relationship with your employees. With employee stock options you can legally maintain a right of first refusal, holding the first right to buy back the shares if the employee leaves or is terminated.

While there are many advantages to a company offering stock options, be careful not to give out options too easily, too quickly, or to persons whose true expertise and loyalty has not been fully demonstrated. What may not seem to cost you much early on in the business could cost you dearly in terms of money and time later on, should your relationship with stock option holders deteriorate.

The lure of stock options is often a major lure for attracting talent to start-up companies in new technology industries.

Companies can formally set up ESOPs (as they are called) to not only raise capital, but also raise employee morale and productivity. In a typical ESOP the employee is allowed, as determined by management, to purchase up to a certain amount of stock during a certain period of time. There are generally regulations about cashing in (redeeming) the stock if the employee should leave the company. An example might see an employee being able to have five percent or more of his or her weekly salary deducted for stock purchase after one year of employment.

The usual benefits to the company include a steady flow of additional capital without having to put up collateral and without needing to pay a set amount of interest. As stockholders, employees see a possible additional source of income that they will have influence over through the quality and productivity of their work.

ESOPs should be handled by an attorney to assure the documentation and communication are done properly, insuring employee confidence in the ESOP and in the company.

Locating Private Resources

Just as it has been in the past, reality suggests that the world of private investors, including friends, relatives, coworkers, wealthy acquaintances (angels) and various sophisticated individual investors are likely places to go to raise capital for your business. The total pool of all types of private investments in business is vast.

Choosing this private path leads to questions of how to find and inform a sufficient pool of potential investors about your need for private funding. Then, in exchange for the investors' money, what mechanism should be used to issue to them the documentation or securities that represent some equity or debt interest in your business? The key is knowing what aspects of deals are critical to your business and having multiple options available as you search for and enter into your funding negotiations.

Next to personal savings, the second most popular source for start-up capital is friends and family. Often, they may not be as worried about quick returns as other outside investors would be. There have been many success stories from investments of friends and family. There is also a high incidence of problems associated with this source.

To illustrate this point, suppose that from the start of your business you had access to only the best and most sophisticated investors. Through this process both the investors and you would develop an understanding of the risks involved with investing in your business. It would be in both your interest and the investor's best interest for you to disclose fully in writing the risks associated with the investment.

Because this process of due diligence is often not carried out with family and friends, problems sometimes ensue. Thus, receiving capital from such a consenting, informed investor is often better than from a rich, unsophisticated relative or friend. Your relative or friend may not investigate your deal carefully and, should problems occur with the business and investment, your relationship with them may suffer.

A wise policy is to provide the same disclosure to a friend or relative that you would provide to most sophisticated investors. Resist the temptation to keep things loose and undocumented. Draw up the terms, conditions and payment schedule in writing for their signature and yours. Even if you receive a friendship loan at no or low interest, provide documentation in return. This is the smart, professional business approach that minimizes the potential down side of unstated assumptions and their implications. As a result of formalizing your deal, your relationship with your friends and family will have a much better chance of remaining intact.

In many ethnic communities and foreign countries private loan clubs are a variation on obtaining funds from friends and family. Often a group of trusted friends pools money monthly to be awarded to a group member who needs and deserves it.

If you are a small business and you only need limited amounts of capital, seeking the type of private investor called an angel might be the best alternative. Over 700,000 angels invest over $30 billion of equity in small businesses each year. These people generally invest in the $25,000 to $50,000 range, but sometimes you can get more by dealing with several angels at once, since they sometimes prefer to invest as a group.

Be sure to check out their resumes and two or three references, especially the names of other entrepreneurs the angel has previously financed. Your angel could be your lawyer, doctor, accountant, or an interested individual in your community or industry. They are often executives who have been successful in an industry and now look to fund other companies in that area. Generally it is best to offer an angel straight equity, part ownership in your business in the form of common stock. Keep it simple and completely spelled out.

Angels have sometimes been called the invisible segment of the venture capital industry. Networking through trade associations, civic organizations and your business community may lead you on the path to an interested angel. With individuals you have a tremendous amount of leeway in structuring the investment. You can structure it as debt or equity and vary the terms and repayment. Sources of personal investors go beyond family and friends.

Your employer may not want to lose your abilities and contributions, should you decide to start your own business. There are situations where this employer can become your first major customer. This can be solidified with a purchase order if you are going to be providing manufactured goods, and also a specifically worded work for hire agreement if you are to provide services to your past employer.

In another situation, your employer may agree with you that it would be wise to spin off an idea of yours into a new company. Providing funds in this type of venture of yours may be a sound investment for the employer, who should already know the market, the competition and your abilities and motivation.

Should this setting unfold, have the appropriate agreements drawn up and signed to protect both sides with regards to resource requirements, payment and delivery. Make sure the employer is made aware of any negative impact the new venture could have on their existing business.

Some additional words of caution: Don't become too dependent on your past employers and don't expect them to do all that it takes to set up your business. You need to start, run and be financially responsible for your company. Also, should your employer not express the interest to help start, fund or continue funding your new business, ask for a signed statement to that effect. At the same time, to be safe, be able to prove that you developed the concept for your business on your own time and with your own resources.

Partnerships are a way to join forces with one or more individuals to expand the capabilities of the business. Like a marriage, the partners bring different and hopefully complementary resources to the business. For example, one may bring technical expertise, while the other may bring the primary financial resources. Another desirable match may be to team a person who has administrative abilities with a person who has strategic vision.

Know your potential partner well before committing to such a business relationship. Ask hard questions. Make sure the agreement is documented clearly and reviewed or drafted by a competent partnership attorney. Exit strategies and procedures for either partner should be detailed in writing early on to avoid conflicts or confusion later on. Communication between partners is crucial for defining the specific roles each partner is to provide to the business, preventing wasteful overlap of activities or gaps in the execution of functions. Honesty and openness with both good and bad news will allow the business to have the best chance at a healthy life.

A partnership can be a way to get a business up and running while one or both partners still have other work or business commitments. It may also be effective in the early stages of business growth or in turnaround situations.

In an effort to quickly put together a profitable project, it is becoming more commonplace to have two or more enterprises join forces for collaborative work in a strategic alliance. With businesses becoming more complex and global every day, and with increased emphasis on specialized knowledge and on fast new product development, partnerships are increasingly emerging among companies and entrepreneurs. The movie industry has modeled the concept of strategic alliances for decades. Diverse talent is sought and brought together for a common, defined project. After the movie is completed, many contributing elements to the production are quickly disbanded.

For this type of shared resource alliance to work consistently, the participating companies must build a high level of trust in each other. Strategic alliances and partnerships are often difficult to coordinate and even harder to control. Should you or any of your strategic partners miss a significant milestone, you may lose your market lead, or even your company or significant parts of it. The relationships between the allied companies need a strong foundation and the goals and values of the companies need to be compatible.

With determination and the ability to prove that a charitable investment in your enterprise will have positive social impact, benefiting more than just you, finding funding from a private, nonprofit foundation is possible. While some foundations fund entrepreneurs directly, most foundations give money and support services to nonprofit organizations, which seek to accomplish the foundation's mission by coordinating and supervising the distribution of these resources in exchange for the specialized work needed.

State or national charitable organizations channel funding from private foundations, as do churches, school groups, art societies and other community organizations. Check your local library for reference books on funding research resources. Once you have identified appropriate foundations or nonprofit organizations request their application guidelines and their annual reports. Then be prepared to spend time and effort filling out paperwork, writing a proposal and business plan and pitching the right people.

In the United States, there are only two ways to legally offer (sell) the securities of your company to investors. 1) The transaction must either be registered with the Securities and Exchange Commission, as is done when a company goes public in the traditional sense, or 2) it must be exempt from SEC registration, often referred to as a private placement or limited stock offering. Due to the considerable legal requirements and the large commitment of time and money involved with a registered Wall Street public offering, many companies may not be ready to go public, and others may not ever want or need to do it. In recent times exempt offerings are becoming more viable alternatives for companies in search of early funding.

McCain's Maxim #8: It's all too easy to underestimate how much money your business will need, especially over the five year planning horizon. But estimate it you must. The National Federation of Independent Business says that over the lifetime of a business, 39 percent are profitable, 30 percent break even, and 30 percent lose money, with one percent falling in the "unable to determine" category.[4] Inadequate financing problems are often the core reason.

---

[4]http://www.businessweek.com/smallbiz/news/coladvice/ask/sa990930.htm

CHAPTER EIGHT

Apply Responsive Accounting Procedures

They Reveal the Company's Strengths and Weaknesses

There are several common financial reports used to inform management of the results of operations, but the most commonly used ones are the balance sheet and the profit & loss statement. These are the two most important documents dealing with the company's financial condition.

Balance Sheet

The balance sheet summarizes the end results of the company's operations from the day the company is organized until the date that the balance sheet is prepared. The balance sheet is divided into three major sections: Assets (what the company owns); Liabilities (what the company owes); and Stockholder's Equity (what the stockholders invested to start the company with the gain or loss since inception).

The balance sheet shows the way a company's assets are balanced against its liabilities plus stockholder's equity. Assets are everything a company owns and liabilities are everything it owes. stockholder's equity is what is left over for the stockholder once everything is paid from what the company owes.

The balance sheet summarizes the condition of the company's assets, liabilities and stockholder's equity at a given point in time; usually the last day of the month for each reporting period and the last day of the fiscal year. The company selects a fiscal year (twelve-month period) as its standard period for annual reporting. This twelve-month period can be the same as the calendar year from January 1 through

December 31, or it can be any other twelve-month period as deemed appropriate by the stockholders. Some companies set their fiscal year at the slowest time of the company's year so that they can have more time to complete the end of year records and activities. The balance sheet normally provides comparison data for the previous year in addition to the current year.

The overall organization of the items on the balance sheet follows standard accounting conventions. The most common organization is to arrange items from top to bottom in a single list with assets listed first, then liabilities and finally stockholder's equity. Most balance sheets normally list assets in the order in which they can be turned into cash. There are four major categories of assets that can be listed on the balance sheet:

Current assets include cash and any other assets that can be turned into cash in the normal operating cycle of the business, which is one year. Following is a listing of items that normally make up current assets:

Petty cash. Cash kept at the office

Checking/savings accounts. Represents money in the bank(s) resulting from all deposits and less all disbursements by check

Other current assets.

Deposits/prepaid expenses. Deposits are often required when leases are signed. They generally represent one to two months cost. Occasionally, items are prepaid and are initially handled as an asset until the charge is transferred to the profit and loss account. For example, real estate tax is paid twice a year covering a six month period. When the payment is made it is all charged to the prepaid real estate tax account.

Other assets are the next category of assets listed on the balance sheet. This category includes any investment the company plans to hold for more than one year, normally for an extended number of years, e.g. stocks, bonds, government securities, or any other asset acquired for investment purposes rather than for short term use. Other assets might include intangible assets that have no distinct form such as goodwill, patents, and copyrights.

Fixed assets are sometimes called property, plant and equipment, or buildings and equipment. This category consists of the actual physical property which in most cases represents a major part of the company's wealth and is normally much more difficult to liquidate (sell) than current assets. These accounts represent the value of capitalized equipment, furniture and fixtures. What is capitalized is established with your accountant. The accountant can generally provide you with guidelines and can be consulted if there is a question. This category can be made up of several different categories such as buildings and equipment, furniture and fixtures and land.

Except for land, all fixed assets have a limited life. Buildings and equipment experience wear as they get older and the real value decreases each year. This decrease is accounted for on the balance sheet as accumulated depreciation, which is defined as the loss in value due to wear and tear. Depreciation is deducted from the original cost to account for the wear and tear.

Each year's depreciation is added to the depreciation of the previous years until an item has been fully depreciated (has no value left on the company's records). The total shown on the balance sheet as accumulated depreciation is deducted from the original cost of buildings and equipment so that the current book value is accurately stated on the balance sheet. (*Note*: Some items may still have value even after they are fully depreciated. If any item appearing on the depreciation schedule is sold, the difference between the selling price and the depreciated book value is reported on the profit & loss statement as a gain or loss from the asset sale.)

Depreciation should be entered using the general journal on a monthly basis. Obtain a copy of the depreciation schedule from the accountant or ask the accountant for an estimate for the year. Divide the total yearly depreciation by 12 and enter this amount each month as follows. If land is listed as a fixed asset; it includes any site(s) used for business purposes. The company may also own other land for investment purposes; however, this land would be listed under other assets.

Liabilities and Stockholder's Equity

This portion of the balance sheet shows the distribution of each dollar of assets to the obligations and ownership of the company. Total liabilities and stockholder's equity is always equal to total assets

The three main categories of information presented on the liabilities and stockholder's equity side of the balance sheet are:

Current Liabilities are short-term debts that must be paid in the next operating period, normally within one year from the date of the balance sheet. They include any short term obligations, e.g. money owed to suppliers for materials and services, dividends due stockholders, salaries, interest or principal payments due on loans and/or notes, federal income taxes, other taxes, and any other payable which will become due in the next year.

Normal categories listed under current liabilities are:

Accounts Payable. All of the currently outstanding short-term debts for goods and services that the company expects to pay within one year following the balance sheet date. When the company purchases goods or services, it does not usually make payment at the time of purchase. Items are normally purchased with terms that always permit a reasonable time period for payment: typically 10, 30, 60 or 90 days.

A vendor (including all relevant information) is established for every payable. A purchase order is created to the supplier for the purchase whenever practical. When an invoice is received, the invoice is compared to the packing list and to the purchase order (if generated). If the amounts are correct, the invoice is entered.

Current Liabilities. These are amounts due but not yet paid for on the balance sheet date, such as federal withholding taxes and accrued FICA. The amounts owed on these items are calculated up to the balance sheet date and are shown on the balance sheet as accrued liabilities. For payroll items, the values are posted to both the expense accounts and to the accrual accounts.

Other Taxes. These may include such items as state franchise taxes, state sales tax collected and payable on items sold that are subject to sales tax.

Notes Payable. This is an IOU. It is a written promise to pay a specific amount at a given date. Notes are classified as current liabilities when they are due to be paid within the next year after the date of the balance sheet. The current year portion of any long term debt can be listed under this category as current portion of long term debt.

Long Term Debt can be several types of debt, e.g. long term borrowing of capital, payment of debts for the purchase of a business. Remember that only debt that will not be paid off within one year of the balance sheet date is included in this category. These are again entered through the general journal. The entries would be the same as shown in the notes payable section above when the item is a bank loan or loan from the owner.

Shareholder Equity can be defined as the 'total' claim of the stockholders against the assets of a company after all liabilities and debts have been paid or another definition would be, it equals the amount of assets remaining after deducting all claims for liabilities and long term debts. Ownership of stock, either common or preferred often represents shareholder equity in a corporation.

Capital Stock. This represents the total dollar value obtained by multiplying the number of shares that have been issued times the par value of each share. Par value is the original face value for each share of stock. This value is an arbitrary dollar amount, which the issuing company assigns when the shares are first issued and has no necessary relationship, at the time of issue or any time later, to the actual value of the shares.

Additional Paid In Capital. The owners may elect to put more money into the business based upon economic conditions or other requirements. This money can either be shown as a loan (long term liability) or as additional paid in capital. This should be checked with the company's accountant at the time that the event occurs to determine the best approach for tax purposes.

Retained Earnings. These are earnings (positive or negative) from previous years that have not been distributed to stockholders as dividends, but have been reinvested in the company.

Net Income. This figure represents the Earnings for the year and is generated by the accounting system from upon the profit & loss statement.

Profit & Loss (Income) Statement

The balance sheet provided one picture of the financial condition of a company. The profit & loss statement provides another picture. The balance sheet presents a picture of the assets, liabilities and ownership of a company at a given point in time; however, it does not provide information about the company's revenues or sales, expenses, or income (loss). The profit & loss statement supplies this type of data. However, unlike the balance sheet, it does not provide information that is frozen for one moment in time and covers multiple years of activity. It represents information for activities, which have occurred over a period of time. The profit & loss statement traces the company's profits and losses over a period of time – the fiscal year. At the end of the fiscal year, when the fiscal year is closed, all profit & loss statement accounts return to zero. The profit & loss statement is an exhibit of the basic equation:
Revenues minus costs and expenses = current income (loss)

The profit & loss statement is organized into five categories of information:
Income (Revenues)

Cost of Sales
Operating Expenses (Overhead)
Other Income/Expenses
Taxes on Income

Inputs to the profit & loss statement should be made on a daily basis so that the profit & loss statement can be generated as soon as possible after the end of the month. This provides management an immediate insight into the total business activities of their company for a one month period of time. The statement normally lists year to date figures as well. Year to date figures are a compilation of all figures for preceding months plus the current month for the current fiscal year. This gives management an insight into the total business activity over an extended period of time. Some profit & loss statements will provide month and year to date figures for the previous year's same periods to allow for comparisons. The profit & loss statement provides management with data that can be used to identify problem areas.

The Income (Revenues) section lists all money received by the company during the profit & loss statement period from the sale of products or services, or from other revenue sources. The company may have any number of categories under this section of the profit & loss statement to reflect the operations of departments.

Cost of Sales normally list the expenses incurred in directly providing the product or service during the profit & loss statement period. The company will have the same departmental categories under this section of the profit & loss statement to reflect the expenses associated with the Income operations as established above.

Typical Variable Accounts in cost of sales:

Wages – direct. Gross wages paid to workers in the plant

Materials-direct. Record materials purchased for contracts

Equipment rental. Costs for equipment rented for production

    All other costs for items purchased or used on contracts goes to the appropriate account in cost of sales. *(Note*: These accounts should be the same as those used for estimating purposes.)

    The accounts described above represent the costs that can be directly associated with performing the service.

    Gross Profit (Loss) is obtained by subtracting the cost of sales total from the income total and represents the contribution to the company from the sale of its products and/or services.

    Expenses (Overhead) are expenses which include salaries of overhead employees, the cost of office operations, depreciation insurance and all other general costs required for operation and management of the business that cannot be directly assigned to department sales. (Expenses must be allocated in a method suitable for the company's operations so that they are included in pricing and breakeven is known for each proposal.) The company may have any number of categories listed under this section. Following are some typical accounts:

Advertising. Record all advertising costs, e.g. radio, TV, and Yellow Pages.

Bank charges. Record all charges levied by banks including bad check fees, and service fees.

Contributions. Record any charitable donations or contributions

    Depreciation. Included in this section are all of the different depreciation expenses. The company accountant may be able to provide the figures to be used, or at least use the numbers from the previous year.

Dues & Subscriptions. Here are all payments for magazines, newspapers, or dues paid for membership in associations.

Equipment Rental Expense. Here are payments for equipment that is rented and used in the office.

Insurance. The following insurance categories may be tracked separately.

General. All insurance payments except worker's compensation.

Workers' Comp. workers' compensation insurance payments.

Health/Medical. This is the company portion for employees. (Employee contributions are credited against this account.)

Interest and Interest Expense is another account listed in this section and represents the cost of financing the company through borrowed funds, i.e. the interest paid on borrowed money. The following Interest categories are tracked separately.

Meals & Entertainment. Here are all expenses for reimbursed meals or entertainment expenses for entertaining customers.

Miscellaneous Expenses. Any expense that does not fall into one of the other categories. *Note:* The value in this account should normally be low. If it is not, there is probably another expense category needed.

Office Supplies. All costs for supplies needed to run the company including paper, ink, and pencils.

Postage. U. S. Postal Service, Federal Express, etc.

Professional Fees. The following categories may be tracked for professional fees:

Accounting Fees paid to outside accountant

Legal   Fees paid to attorneys

Other   Fees paid to consultants

Repairs & Maintenance. Listed here are repairs to the main building, office equipment and vehicles. Includes cleaning expenses paid to outside companies.

Garbage Removal. Here are payments for this service.

Taxes. The following tax categories are tracked.

Property

State Franchise

Telephone. All costs associated with communications including telephone and pagers.

Utilities. Gas, electric, and water. These can be tracked separately if desired by creating sub-accounts.

Wages. Including the following sub-categories:

Wages –Office. Gross Wages paid to all employees.

Wages – FICA Cost of company FICA (Social Security and Medicare) costs for payroll for all employees.

Wages – FUTA. Cost of company federal unemployment tax costs for payroll for all employees.

Wages – SUTA. Cost of company state unemployment tax costs for payroll for all employees.

Operating Profit (Loss) is obtained by subtracting the total operating expense from the gross profit.

Other Income represents money the company receives which is not directly related to the products and/or services provided. Included in this category might be interest earned on savings or checking accounts, gain (loss) on sale of assets, and other like items.

Interest income. Used to record interest on savings accounts or other interest bearing investments.

Other income. Used to record income that does not fall into one of the other categories.

Sale of asset – gain (loss). The company may sell a piece of equipment. If the selling price is greater than the book value (from the depreciation schedule) there is a gain.

Profit before taxes is obtained by adding the other income to the operating profit (loss) and represents the results of the company for the period(s) covered prior to allowance for federal and state corporation taxes.

Taxes on Income and other types of taxes are listed on the balance sheet as current liabilities. The balance sheet shows the total of all types of taxes *owed* as of the balance sheet date. The amount shown is usually less than the total tax expense for the year. This is because taxes are normally paid in installments as the year progresses. Some taxes have already been paid during the year prior to the balance sheet date. The amount shown on the balance sheet will probably be paid in installments after the balance sheet date.

The actual expense of taxes paid during the year is shown on the profit & loss statement. Some types of taxes are included in the figures for operating expenses. The income taxes paid during the year are shown separately on the profit & loss statement in a separate section called income taxes.

Net Income for the period is the most important item of the financial information on the profit & loss statement. It is the key measure of the company's performance – the amount of profit achieved after all costs, expenses and taxes have been paid from revenues.

McCain's Maxim #9 A lack of understanding about accounting, the most fundamental of systems relating to a determining a company's profitability, has assigned what otherwise would have been a money-making enterprise to the dust bin of business history. To quote Bernie Ebbers, former head of bankrupt World Com, from his prison cell, "I know what I don't know. To this day, I don't know technology, and I don't know finance or accounting."

CHAPTER NINE

Control Overhead

Get Your Hands around These Difficult-to-Control Costs

Overhead costs are all incidental operating expenses that cannot be specifically identified and charged to a specific product or service (examples: telephone, office salaries, rent, and office supplies). The term overhead is used interchangeably with burden or indirect expenses. Those expenses that can be identified with a particular job are direct expenses, such as direct material and direct labor.

In the job costing process, overhead must be applied (added to) the direct costs of the specific job by a method determined to be appropriate for the company. The major reason for doing all the work of defining and allocating overhead is to assure company management that all work bid and completed is anchored on accurate product cost.

It is of equal importance to a company that all overhead costs be covered (absorbed) in its pricing/fee structure as it is that every overhead item be charged to the corresponding department or product accurately.

Overhead Expense Accumulation

It is important that overhead formulations and pricing/estimate forms be compatible with company accounting procedures. While it is of great importance to identify, quantify and allocate these incidental expenses, it is questionable whether extreme detail that is a struggle to obtain provides any more accurate product costs then some of the simpler strategies.

Transaction records that become part of the income statement to support expense collection are determined based on accounting needs. Each company must have these records available and assimilated into its overall program before overhead allocation can take place. These records must be current, accurate, and correctly classified into the divisions on the income statement deemed pertinent for this company's method of overhead allocation.

For most operations it is important to decide what portions of these costs are fixed and which are variable. This is especially true if allocations will be predetermined with the budgeting process rather than calculated from actual, after-the-fact collection of support detail. Classification of expenses according to their behavior is of considerable importance in controlling them, developing budgets, calculating predetermined overhead rates and understanding the effect of overhead on their cost.

Once a company is assured that all expenses are captured and classified in as much detail as is important for the specific operation and the income statement produced, any of several ways of allocating   overhead to a product, job or department may be used.

Overhead Application Formulas

Selecting the appropriate formula for use in a given company is totally dependent upon the company's objectives and type of operation. The measures must be commonly used in industry and are actual direct labor hours, direct labor dollars, vehicle or parts cost. Other measures are employed in special applicable situations.

Some criteria that could be used in selecting the most appropriate application are that:

1. The primary productive element (e.g., in the automobile industry, this would be delivered product cost) be utilized as the base in developing the

application rate. That base should relate indirect expenses to the product/service in a logical sense.

2. Separate rates developed for each area that represents a homogeneous cost unit for deriving product costs, i.e. departments, or cost centers.

3. Elimination of unusual fluctuations due to significant volume changes will take place; there will be average rates without seasonal influences.

4. Provision for necessary capability and data to prepare an income statement which realistically represents operational results will be made.

5. Understanding is that departmental or cost centers rates are generally superior to blanket rates because of their greater flexibility to change and use.

Acceptance of the idea that rates based on time (direct labor) are generally preferable to those based on a variable cost factor (labor dollars or material costs) is necessary. This is due to the fact that many expenses are fixed charges which are functions of time (taxes, depreciation, and insurance) and cost factors may not fluctuate with overhead change direction. The method used should be practical, applicable and conducive to the needs of the company.

Shown below are the more common calculation formulas. Any may be used depending on the considerations of the company. Administering many of them depends upon identifying the line items on the income statement that are judged to be overhead dollars are noted. Each of these formula divisions will result in a factor or multiplier that is applied to every job costing effort. This factor is subsequently multiplied by the denominator of the formula to get the overhead cost for an individual job.

For example: $$\frac{\textit{Overhead Dollars}}{\textit{Direct Labor Dollars}}$$

where total *overhead dollars*   = $ 400,000

where *direct labor dollars*   = $1,400,000
then the factor will be $400,000/$1,400,000 = 0.2857

For every dollar of direct labor cost an additional 28.57 cents needs to be added to cover overhead. On a new budget, then, if labor is estimated to be $45,000, an overhead amount of $12,856.50 must be added. ($45,000 * .2859 = $12,856.50).

It is also frequently expedient to use overhead calculated as a percentage of total sales as an allocation factor. For example, if annual sales are $ 4,318,922, and the overhead lines on the income statement total $264,000, the factor/multiplier will be .0612 ($264,000/$ 4,318,922 = .0612). This indicated that for every dollar received in sales 6.12 cents goes to cover overhead. It is necessary to mark-up direct costs by $99,710 to cover the 6.12 percent overhead. Every job estimate using this method must be treated in the same way as above. Adding 6.12 percent to the cost does not yield 6.12 of the amount of sales.

In many operations where labor generates a much greater overhead than any of the other job costs, calculating overhead as a percentage of direct labor using a formula similar to the one exemplified in step 1 above, but in a simpler way, is acceptable.

For example: If overhead is 6.12 percent of sales and direct labor is 60 percent of sales the multiplier will be:

$$\frac{.0612}{.60} = .1020$$

That says for every dollar of labor, another 10.2 cents must be added to cover overhead.

If direct labor is $900, overhead will be $91.80 (900 * .1020 = $91.80). The total job cost calculation before profit could be:

Job Material Cost	$ 993.00
Job Labor Cost	900.00
Job Overhead Cost	91.80
Total Job Cost:	$ 1,884.80

It is plain to see that the more labor generating the overhead the more dollars in overhead are needed, so this can be a sensible approach. The following example shows what happens to the same cost dollars for a job, with less labor.

Job Material Cost	$ 1,100.00
Job Labor Cost	693.00
Job Overhead Cost	70.69
Total Job cost =	$1,863.69

This selection and sampling of overhead application formulas includes the commonly-used ones. Any way that
allows for overhead assignment to a Pricing estimating activity that effectively recognizes the relationships between all the costs can be created for the individual use of a company.

Overhead and Under-Absorbed Overhead
It is one thing to calculate what should be the overhead cost on a given item based on last year's or last period's actual costs or a predetermined overhead rate based on this year's or this period's budget and quite another to track what is happening to make sure the company is on target with all its operations. One of the worst possible scenarios in a business is to plan to make a profit and end up losing money after a period's operation.
Variances from plan must be calculated and problems identified as soon as possible so that corrective action can be taken when necessary or pricing adjusted to become more competitive.
The simplest method to use is a tracking report that lists by month, the amount of overhead absorbed when it is completed. This form also tallies a running total for all months to date. At the top is the amount budgeted to be covered for the entire year. After a few moments review and a quick calculation, management can see how much overhead has been

absorbed to date and whether the company is on, or behind or ahead of schedule.

For example, if on June 30 (six months into the annual period = Fiscal Year, FY), 58 percent of the annual overhead has been absorbed, the company is ahead of schedule. If the company is behind schedule, overhead is not covered and a deficit exists. It is then prudent to include a portion of the deficit on a pro-rated basis *plus* the normal overhead on job estimates or pricing and charge or price until the gap is closed. Not to do so risks the targeted profitability for the year.

If more than the current overhead is covered, it allows future estimates/pricing either greater latitude in pricing or a greater percentage of profit. When this is the case, not only is overhead covered currently, but future overhead is partially covered. The objective is to eliminate overhead each year as rapidly as possible.

A second method also utilizes a tracking report or application summary. The process, however, is based on the concept that a relationship exists between direct costs, indirect costs and general and administrative expense. Direct costs for this purpose can be estimated, measured and billed. Labor and materials, are some examples of these direct costs.

Indirect costs (operating costs) also known as variable overhead, are those costs that are difficult or impossible to determine on a job-to-job basis. Equipment repair, insurance, shop supplies are all elements of indirect cost.

General and administrative (G&A) expenses, also known as fixed overhead, are those expenses not related to service or installation (production), but are not required to run the business. Examples are rent, officers' salaries, and sales expenses

A relationship exists between these components. Based on the period forecast (budget), the total direct costs require a specific amount of indirect costs and G & A expenses. The ratios between total direct costs, indirect costs, and G & A are the overhead recovery rates. This theory demonstrates that this relationship is true for the budgeted values and can now be extended to each individual job.

For example, if the budget says:

Total Direct Labor	$ 53,775
Total Material	225,885
Total Sub-Contract	46,727
	$326,357
Total Indirect Cost	$ 39,410
Total G & A	$132,538

Variable Overhead Recovery Rate (V.O.R.R.) =

$$\text{V.O.R.R.} = \frac{\text{Total Indirect Cost}}{\text{Total Direct Cost}}$$

$$\text{V.O.R.R.} = \frac{\$\,39,410}{\$326,357} = .1208$$

Therefore, for every dollar of direct cost, it takes 12.08 cents to cover indirect (operating) costs. Fixed overhead recovery rate (F.O.R.R.) =

$$\text{F.O.R.R.} = \frac{\text{Total G \& A Expense}}{\text{Total Direct Cost}}$$

$$\text{F.O.R.R.} = \frac{\$\,132,538}{\$\,326,357} = .4061$$

For every dollar of direct cost, it takes 40.61 cents to cover General and Administrative cost. The tracking report simply captures Indirect and G & A expenses separately. The difference between the selling price less the direct costs less indirect allocation, less G & A expenses may be considered profit at this point, or it can be applied to the G & A expenses. Recording this additional amount to G & A allows management to track the fixed overhead until it is fully absorbed and the company begins to accrue true annual profit.

The indirect (variable) overhead must be applied even after the G & A has been absorbed. This is because these costs always occur as direct costs are incurred. G & A (fixed) stops after the annual cost is paid.

Once all the overhead has been absorbed, pricing on bids can be done as usual with overhead and profit added. It can be done with only indirect and profit added or it can be done with lowered G & A profit. It depends on the company strategy, goals, and how badly a specific customer is desired.

Disposition of the final (annual) variance on the income statement is dependent upon various factors. If the amount is small, it is usually carried under other income or expense accounts on the income statement. Further, if the variances are significant, it indicates that overhead and/or production estimates were considerably in error. In these circumstances, adjustments are made to the cost of sales and inventory in the same ratio that the overhead cost was initially applied.

McCain's Maxim #10: Try this three-prong approach to controlling overhead costs. First, identify them to their lowest common denominator. For example, don't lump overtime costs into the more generic labor costs; separate them and track their costs against budget. Second, calculate variances on a timely basis. For example, it's best to control overtime costs on a daily basis rather than wait to the end of the month to detect unfavorable variances. Third, take aggressive corrective action to reduce the overhead expense.

CHAPTER TEN

Calculate Variances to Plan
and Take Corrective Action

They Help Change Course When Problems Occur

A business traveler told me this story one rainy Friday afternoon in O'Hare as we were awaiting our weather-delayed flights home:

"The first job I had right out of college, salesman for a large consumer products company, lasted six months, The company I worked for shut down my division and I was left suddenly unemployed.

"I scrambled around to find a job and got lucky. A local entrepreneur whose small toy manufacturing business was slowing down needed a hot shot salesperson to spur growth. I was young and ready to accept any challenge. I got the offer and started work.

"I immediately hit the large chain stores and was able to sell them on our line of toys. Business almost tripled overnight and the factory scrambled to produce all the toys my customers were ordering.

"The guy I worked for, the founder and chief executive, was nothing if not brilliant. His designs were better than almost anything on the toy market at the time. Unfortunately, he was not as well versed on running a business as he was on designing the product. And he didn't understand how to control operations. So, wisely, he hired an outside accountant to set up an expense and control procedure based on identifying and analyzing cost variances.

*"But my boss had his head in the clouds. He was
already busy designing products for another one of his
businesses and neglected the variance procedure for the toy
company. He was also headstrong and refused to delegate any
real authority, so the control of expenses went by the wayside.*

*"I'm sure you can see what's coming. We had all the
orders we could handle and then some, but costs were wildly
out of control. Profits dropped into negative territory and a
cash crisis followed. The bank closed the business and I was
once again out on the street."*

A financial plan is worthless without the means to see if
it's adhering to plan. That's the purpose of the budget variance
report, which compares actual business results with projections
taken from the budget. Variance analysis is a means of
providing management with a tool by which it can compare
actual operating results to the budget on a periodic basis and
discover which expense items deviate significantly from
forecast. Management can then investigate the reason for the
variance and take swift action to prevent its recurrence.

Variance analysis must be performed no later than on a
monthly basis so that problems causing variances can be
identified and dealt with before they negatively and
substantially impact the P&L, rather than being allowed to
persist. The earlier on a problem is discovered, the more time
the company has to overcome the negative variance.

In many instances variances to plan are calculated
weekly, sometimes daily, and in a system called short-interval
scheduling, hourly. But the shorter intervals are normally used
to measure production variances of discrete units. For purposes
of this examination, we're talking dollars.

The monthly variance report must be completed by the
controller on the first business day after the monthly income
statement is available. This means the report should be
completed by the seventh working day of the next month. This
assures that this report is given the necessary priority. It will
also assure that appropriate measures, as required, are

immediately implemented to eliminate variances. Finally, it guarantees that variance discussions take place soon enough after the analysis occurrences to be certain that managers can remember the causes.

Calculate Variances to Plan

The variance report consists of the listing of expense classifications as shown here: forecast, actual, standard cost, and monthly variance, quarterly variance, and year-to-date variance.

Forecast: Enter the forecasted sales volume and the expense amounts for each item at that sales volume from the budgeted amount.

Actual: At the end of each month, the actual revenues and expenses for the month are recorded.

*Standard Cost***:** This cost reflects the standard cost adjusted to the current volume of sales.

Monthly Variance: Standard minus actual cost. Be sure to note negative results in red ink or brackets.

Quarterly Variance: The total of the variances for the current quarter.

Year-to-date Variance: The total of the variances for the fiscal year-to-date.

A copy of the variance report is given to the owner or president each month upon its completion. During the ensuing review by the owner or president with department heads, particular attention must be given to any negative variances and reasons for these variances must be determined in order to initiate corrective action.

The investigation of a variance from standard may indicate that the standard is unreasonable. If any budgeted standard proves to be too high or too low over a period of time, an adjustment can be made by the owner or president or other manager responsible for setting budget parameters.

It is important to remember that while the budget is the company's target, variances will always exist to some degree. This does not mean that management should consider them tolerable or inevitable. *Although zero variances are not always achievable, they should be the goal.* There will always be one or more explanations for every variance.

The company should focus only on those variances that are significant. Normally, only expense items with variances of 20 percent or more will be discussed during the review. If management finds few items with this large a variance, it may reduce the number to 10 percent. The percentage can be adjusted higher or lower as needed.

Revenue variances are analyzed differently from expense variances. For one thing, Revenue is one area where exceeding the budget is a good thing and falling short of the budget is bad. Revenue variances must be analyzed to determine why they occurred, particularly if revenues were less than the budgeted goal.

If revenues fall short because of a lack of business, this issue must be addressed. The entire budget depends upon meeting or exceeding sales goals. Fixed expense levels are set based on a budgeted Revenue amount. If sales fall short of goals, the budget is faced with an immediate handicap that is difficult to overcome. Even if all expenses are within budget, a revenue shortfall can prevent the company from achieving its profit objective.

If sufficient business exists but revenues fall short, the company has either a productivity problem or insufficient staffing. If the direct labor numbers are within budget, the problem is a lack of workers. If the direct labor numbers have a significant negative variance, the problem is productivity. The reasons for the productivity problems must be satisfactorily explained by the managers. Whether the problem is lack of material, labor inefficiencies, or other problems, a corrective action plan must be created to assure the problem does not continue or repeat itself.

If revenues are short of budgeted goals, management must determine which of three conditions exist before going forward. If the ensuing months are also expected to fall short of revenue goals, management must scrutinize the fixed expenses, and determine areas of possible reduction. If all expense numbers meet budget but revenues fall short, the company will not meet desired profit goals. If the ensuing months are expected to be back on track, the shortfall has been remedied, but annual totals will be impacted by the shortfalls that already occurred. The ideal situation is if the company can beat the revenue goal in the ensuing months to overcome the existing shortfall. However, this catch-up must be accomplished without an associated increase in cost of sales percentage or fixed expenses. Otherwise, variances will be created in expense items. Therefore, use of overtime may not be the ideal way to correct revenue shortfalls.

Cost of sales items are compared to the levels they should be based on actual sales. Therefore, revenue fluctuations are never an acceptable explanation for variances in these items. If these variances occur, the reasons are strictly pertaining to operational efficiencies.

If revenues are below budget, cost of sales expenses should be lowered proportionately. The only exception is if inventories are higher than normal. If this variance occurs, it is not due to the lack of sales, but because of management's failure to respond to the lack of sales.

An increase in sales volume over budget levels is not a justification for an increase in cost of sales as a percentage of sales. The increased business must be properly planned. If the increases are expected to be permanent, the company must staff itself accordingly, not work overtime. Even if increases in business are expected to be temporary, there are less expensive alternatives than overtime. It is the responsibility of management to assure that staffing levels are appropriate and that the schedule can be accomplished without overtime.

Every expense item should have one person who is responsible for it. In the case of cost of sales items, this will be the buyer of the items. Most of the fixed expense accounts are managed by the controller. The person responsible for an account should be the person responsible for the items that go into the account. This person will be asked to explain any variances.

There are many common reasons for variances. They include omission of an item during creation of the budget, one-time unanticipated expenses, entry of an expense item into the wrong account, timing issues, increases or decreases in efficiency or productivity, or unrealistic goal setting by management.

A determination must be made as to whether a variance is recurring or a one-time occurrence. Recurring variances are generally of greater concern since they will impact performance against budget each time they occur.

If different one-time occurrences repeatedly impact the budget, and they are significant, unavoidable, and unforeseeable, an allowance must be made for them when budgeting.

A variance may occur because the budget goals were unrealistic. If this is the case, the budget should be modified to more accurately coincide with reality. However, management should only revise budget goals if they are absolutely unattainable. management should be reluctant to accept inaccurate budgeting as a variance explanation.

Timing issues can cause variances because some expenses do not occur evenly during the year from month to month. As the year progresses, the year-to-date variances on those items will shrink. If they do not, there are other factors besides timing contributing to the variance.

Variance may occur because of inconsistencies in the classification of expenses. Care must be taken to preserve the integrity of the accounts. As previously mentioned, the controller must create and maintain a detailed list of what expense items are charged to which accounts. All employees involved in assigning account codes must have a copy of this list. This will become important once you institute the accounting program we have discussed.

Variances may occur because of an oversight during the budgeting process. If this is the case, the budget must be modified to account for the omitted items.

Variances may occur simply because of poor performance against the budget. It is the responsibility of every manager to control the accounts under his domain. If poor performance is the reason for the variance, the manager responsible needs to develop a specific plan for improvement. Continued poor performance should prompt management to take appropriate steps. Tolerance of poor performance will produce recurring poor performance.

In general, management must be very intolerable of variances to the budget. Variances are deviations from the path to the profit goal. A ten dollar variance of a fixed expense costs the company ten dollars in profit. management needs to ask itself if it was worthwhile to spend ten dollars from profit on the variance.

Any items with large variances that have not been satisfactorily explained must be more closely tracked in the following months to assure its return to conformity with the budget.

Year-to-date variance analysis is helpful in identifying trends or persistent variances that are not improving over time. A negative variance of a significant nature that occurs month after month is symptomatic of poor budgeting or lack of control. An item that varies from positive to negative month to month may just be subject to timing issues.

It is important that the person responsible for particular expense items be involved in setting the goals during the budgeting process. This will make her less apt to invoke incorrectly budgeting amounts as the cause of any variances. It also enables management to hold him accountable. Managers cannot reasonably be held accountable for failure to meet goals they did not help set. Although the other employees, such as the service manager, may have input, ultimately the president or chief financial officer must determine the final number. They should obtain concurrence from the responsible employee.

As management becomes accustomed to the budgeting and variance reporting process, budgeting accuracy should improve and variances should decrease. The more accurate the budget, the more useful a tool it becomes.

It is important to examine substantial positive variances as well as negative ones rather than to just attribute them to good fortune. A positive variance may occur because needed expenditures were not made. For example, failure to purchase needed and budgeted safety supplies can cause a positive variance in the short term. But if an accident occurs because of the lack of this supply, workers compensation rates will rise, costing the company money and creating a more significant negative variance.

If a positive variance is due to an improvement in efficiency or productivity, or some other improvement, it is important that the company discover the reasons to assure that the variance continues. If the reason for the variance is not determined, the variance will likely disappear. Permanent improvements should be incorporated into future budgets.

Care must be taken not to attribute a variance wholly to a factor that might be the cause of only part of the variance. For example, a variance in employee labor might be only 20 percent attributable to overtime resulting from a major project, or the something as simple as a shop lead being on vacation. Yet a manager might use that explanation as the reason for the entire variance. Managers must have documented information to support their variance explanations.

If many expense items persist in having negative variances month after month, this is indicative of the budget being too ambitious. On the contrary, if many expense items have significantly positive variances month after month, management has set the goals too low.

While monthly variances are certainly significant, the year-to-date numbers have greater importance. Monthly spikes are less of a problem if they average out over time, and variances for the year to date are small or non-existent.

Corrective Action Mode

Corrective action planning is a tool for continuous improvement. The objective of a corrective action plan is to define the corrective action, assign responsibility for implementation and provide for follow-up.

A corrective action plan is used to eliminate an unfavorable variance or to sustain a favorable variance. It has several parts. Each part must be included if the plan is to be effective. The parts are:

Statement of Problem. Describe the problem.

Root Cause. The root cause of the variance must be identified. This is usually done as a committee of the parties involved based on studies performed by engineers or others assigned to determine causes of the problem.

Plan of Action. This is the plan developed by the group as to the method of eliminating the variance.

Responsible Party. Assigning the party responsible for the implementation is an important step not to be neglected.

Suspense Date. The date the action plan is to be completed demands rigorous follow-up.

Follow Up. The person responsible for following up to assure that the plan is implemented must be identified.

Form Used. The plan does not need to elaborate. A simple form like the one following is appropriate.

VARIANCE CORRECTIVE ACTION PLAN

Prepared by: _____ Date: _____

Statement of problem:
_____
_____
_____
_____

Root cause identified:
_____
_____
_____
_____
_____

Corrective action:
_____
_____
_____
_____
_____

Assigned to for implementation:
_____

Follow up by: _____
Results:
_____
_____
_____
_____

McCain's Maxim #11: Cash and profits are the lifeblood of a company, the friendly forces. Costs are the enemy. You must defeat the enemy to remain in business. A disciplined variance analysis procedure

combined with an effective corrective action program that identifies and eliminates root causes of problems will help assure your company's permanence.

CHAPTER ELEVEN

Improve Productivity

Productivity Must Improve Every Year
Because Costs Increase Every Year

Listen in on this conversation between Ken, a management trainer, and Ralph, a new supervisor, talking about productivity:

"Ken, I understand the need to improve productivity, but I don't understand the need to improve it constantly, year after year."

"Good point, Ralph, and the answer is quite simple. Look at costs of your parts and materials and supplies. They tend to go up every year, even in a down economy. So do the costs of your company's services. Chances are your company's labor costs do, too. In fact, increasing company costs is a constant."

Ralph nods. "I'm getting your point."

"That upward cost pressure must be relieved or a company will eventually go bankrupt."

"The way you put it, Ken, that means managers must always be looking for ways to decrease costs."

"Exactly. And there are only a few ways to do this: cut overhead costs, redesign the product or service for more efficient delivery, reduce inventory, increase throughput, or reduce labor costs. That kind of thing."

"I guess what you're getting at is that productivity improvements are one of the best ways to cut costs."

"If you can do the same amount of work with fewer employees or find a way to increase throughput with your existing workforce, those are productivity improvements that go right to the bottom line."

"How about cutting unanticipated costs such as overtime?"

"Another good example. Ralph we could sit here all day and talk about ways to decrease costs. The best way to approach it is to get everybody involved in cost reduction, from the worker on the floor to the company executives. Cost reduction is every employee's business."

"Time to get busy, I guess."

"I couldn't have said it better. Time to get busy."

Labor Productivity

The procedure outlined below is designed to provide a method to measure the productivity levels of labor in the shop environment.

Labor is an expensive commodity to any operation. The control of labor cost should be one of utmost concern to any business owner. Having a method to measure the effectiveness of your labor dollar is very important to controlling the cost of labor.

Labor productivity is the amount of work obtained for the hours that are incurred. Simply, the value you receive from the dollars you spend on labor. There are many methods that can measure productivity. Several require intricate formulas and methods to determine productivity. *The simplest methods to measure productivity are often the best.*

The essence of this system is designed to reflect the efficiency of shop labor, using previous jobs as a guide to man-hours for productivity, and a comparison of actual labor hours and costs from payroll, contrasted with the cost standards for each product, which will be the basis for valuating production efficiency in the evaluation of labor hours on each job run, and for estimating new jobs which have historical data that will be used to price new orders.

The man-hours and costs collected and presented in labor tracking reports will reflect the actual labor hours for the product, which should then be compared to previous the labor costs for previous periods. This will enable the supervisor to measure the performance of his department to see if productivity is in line.

The payroll data for shop labor is compared to the actual hours coded to jobs for the time period in a report designed to give the shop supervisor a picture of the amount of labor hours that are being spent indirectly on tasks such as cleaning, maintenance or any other purpose that is not a direct charge to a production run and captured on a labor tracking form.

Labor hours for each job, with product code designations, are submitted as each job run is completed in the shop. Accounting takes the data labor tracking sheets furnished by the shop supervisor and enters it on a spreadsheet designed to produce the productivity cost report. This report has historical data with man-hours by product type. A separate spreadsheet is created which shows the comparison and variations for recent job orders, which are submitted to the shop supervisor. He then evaluates the results and uses this data as a guide to spot any deterioration in performance by employees, and determine if the variances are justified due to special problems relating to a specific order, or if there are reasons that dictate new standards for a given product. In that case, a revised standard would need to be coordinated with estimating so that new pricing can be implemented for future jobs.

Utilizing the same source document—the labor tracking form—total man-hours for the pay period are accumulated and entered into the labor efficiency report. Separate entries in the report are the total hours paid for shop employees during that pay period. The difference between the two, and the percentage of labor charged to jobs produced, denotes the percentage of time the employees are spending on indirect activities. If a budget is prepared with an annual estimate of the time allotted for these indirect tasks, this ratio would also be reflected in the report. Variances from the budget, and a trend of the ratios of such labor hours per unit will aid the shop supervisor in his monitoring of the percentage of labor spent for indirect tasks.

Labor hours per unit of product are expected to vary from small orders to larger orders, as efficiency improves in volume production. However, other factors can influence the per unit numbers, such as new employees who are not trained properly or who are not as proficient as they should be, to other problems ranging from disruptions in work flow and more. The standards developed over time will be the guide for man-hour and cost formulas which will be the basis for estimating and bottom line profits. If the actual hours per unit do not perform according to plan, management needs to know, and if corrective action is required, after analysis of the problem, the variances point the way. If there are fundamental reasons why the labor has increased, or decreased, and is expected to be the new norm, this is also a necessary piece of information which will be critical to scheduling the production, and to estimating, as the new cost formula is put into the equation for new job estimates.

Non-productive labor is a necessary evil, as maintenance and repair work is performed, inventories are taken, walls are painted, all sorts of activity the company pays the employee to perform, but that is not used on a given job order in a direct/productive manner. This ratio of man-hours, indirect labor, should be budgeted and become a planned factor in the labor burden equation for cost estimate purposes. It is also a guide for the shop supervisor as an expected amount of lost time that will occur over the course of the year. However, this ratio must be monitored to assure that the predicted rate is not being exceeded, otherwise, the true cost absorbed by the company is not totally reflected in the burden rate used to cost out a job. Again, such an event would result in lost profits, due to an imprecise cost estimate. This is a never ending battle to control the labor cost in order to remain competitive.

Note that significant discrepancies in this ratio may indicate that there are inefficiencies in the operation, that supervision of the labor force may be inadequate, or that procedures and techniques in the tasks that are performed need to be reviewed, modified, and improved.

High productivity provides profitable operations. Increasing labor costs or reducing the ability to service customers in a timely manner results in losses of profit to a business. A method to measure productivity must be used daily so that management can know how productive the shop is. Productivity can only be improved when management sets a realistic standard and quickly reacts to the standard not being met.

Sales Productivity

The following procedure provides management with the detail necessary to measure individual salesperson efficiency.

There are at least six different considerations that can be taken into account when determining individual sales employees' efficiencies:

The percent of the total sales force effort the salesperson has/is generating.

The number of calls the salesperson has made within a given period of time and the sales dollars that have been generated per call. This may be broken down into cold calls (in person or by phone), leads followed up in person or by phone, and repeat business.

The sales dollars that have been generated for each dollar in salary the salesperson is paid.

The dollars of old business that the salesperson generates.

The dollars of new business the salesperson generates.

The dollars of repeat business the salesperson generates.

The measures of performance listed above may be weighted for periods of time or by product lines. management may want to target repeat business or business in older sales territories and will give added weight to the sales dollar obtained in that market segment.

An accurate account of each salesperson's effort must be maintained before the performance measures can be determined. (See Form A at the end of this section.) Additionally, accurate job and product costs must also be available.

The salesperson's effort as a percent of the total sales force effort is determined by dividing the total sales dollars that have been generated (not the total sales dollars which might include counter sales and in-house sales. unless that is a part of the force being measured), into the dollars that were generated by the salesperson: Example:

Total budgeted sales dollars for salesperson= $55,000 during the month

Total actual dollars sold for the month= $23,515

Salesperson's efficiency measurement= 42.8 percent ($23,515/$55,000)

Each salesperson must keep a record of all calls that they have made. This record must be turned over to the vice president of sales at the end of each designated period. The data are then verified (actual sales generated, some random call backs, and so on). The total number of sales dollars generated by the salesperson is divided by the total number of calls the salesperson made. This is only an indicator of activity and can be used to help increase sales by determining that not enough calls are being made. However, only total sales made are the measures of performance.

The total dollars that a salesperson is paid, including items like car allowance, insurance, and expense totals for the period are divided into the total sales dollars (or profit dollars if you are using profit as a baseline) that the salesperson has generated:

Total dollars sold:
$23,515

Total wages paid
$13,225

Sales dollar per cost dollar
$23,515/$13,225 = $1.78

This may be looked at as gross margin profit, or, when real profit and job cost information are available, real profit.

The dollars of new business generated is the total dollars of business that the salesperson has sold during this period. A time frame of years may be desired to accurately define new business. The dollars of repeat business generated are the total dollars of business the salesperson has sold within the past year.

There are several ratios that can be used to measure salesperson's efficiency in addition to the actual dollar volume of sales that the salesperson generated. These ratios, just as straight dollar volumes generated, can then be compared to the attainments of other salespersons. These measurements should be used to help a failing salesperson to redirect sales efforts, as well as to aid in determining incentives.

The best determination of the individual value of a salesperson is to compare the return on investment in that salesperson. This can only be determined if accurate recording, costing and profit data are being captured and maintained.

FORM (A)

SALES - DAILY CALL REPORT

Name	Telephone	Comments
-----	-----	-----
-----	-----	-----
-----	-----	-----
-----	-----	-----
-----	-----	-----
-----	-----	-----
-----	-----	-----
-----	-----	-----

Use the COMMENTS section to record the dollar amounts of any sales made, verbal notes for yourself, and the following: CB= call back, NA= no answer , VIP= very interested person, UR= use as reference, PC= previous customer.

Employee Teams

There is a general consensus in modern American business today that the most effective manner to increase productivity is through employee participation.

A basic method of involving employees is through

productivity teams where employees are divided into teams responsible for improving productivity. Employees set their own goals and are encouraged to develop their own methods to reach them. This concept is based on four assumptions:

Individuals will put forth more effort to achieve goals they have helped to create.

An atmosphere of cooperation already exists among employees working on individual teams.

Employees will act positively or negatively, depending on their perceived compatibility with company goals and objectives,

Voluntary commitment to these goals is essential to both job satisfaction and increased productivity.

Before a company can move forward toward the team concept, it must determine whether it can be applied successfully in its existing atmosphere. Some managerial styles do not allow the acceptance of teamwork. However, even if Senior Management thinks the work force would adapt to a teamwork concept, a test program will provide the real answer.

The simplest way to test acceptance of the team concept is to form an employee advisory council. This group is designed to present suggestions to management concerning problems, which they perceive. The various departments of the company would each be asked to elect a representative to serve on the council for a period no to exceed six months. These elected members should not be in supervisory or management positions.

Managers would also be asked to elect a representative to serve on the committee. The council would be asked to meet every other week and provide suggestions for improvement of operations, methods and procedures of the company.

The council should understand that its existence is for the primary purpose of making recommendations and not policy. The company's only commitment to this council is to guarantee a response to any suggestions submitted, positive or negative.

After the council has existed for a reasonable period (two to three months,) management will be able to consider if it has been effective. The effectiveness will not necessarily be judged on what the council produced in suggestions, (however telling this may be,) but on the cooperative manner by which it maintained itself. The feedback received, the commonality of understanding as to its purpose, and presentation of real as opposed to perceived problems, of course, will be the true keys to its effectiveness.

Teams are to be established throughout the organization at each successive level. Recommendations would be made at the lowest level, reviewed by the next highest team level and added to or eliminated. After reaching the highest level, approved recommendations travel back down for implementation.

Teams of three to eight employees are established within each department, with a supervisor who serves as a team leader and facilitator. The structure and size of teams depends upon the size of the department and the company. In a small company, departments may be combined to form a team.

On the next level, supervisors participate as team members, with the department head serving as the team leader. Department heads, conversely, participate on the next level as members with the owner or manager acting as the team leader.

Initially, teams should meet frequently (every two weeks,) but eventually, as the number of subjects to be addressed is reduced, meetings can be held monthly.

Initially, Managers should attend several meetings where the company communicates the broad corporate objectives (goals) of improved productivity or profitability. These goals may take the form of percentage increase in the volume level or a percentage of the anticipated growth. Goals are then established for each individual team and distributed to the team leader responsible.

Ample information from all organizational levels should be distributed to the team leaders, including data on market conditions, product changes, employees, budgets, and historical volume records. The idea is to have an informed team.

The greatest demand of this process is placed upon the team leaders. It is their responsibility to foster full participation while still keeping focus on the productive issues. In a non-authoritarian manner they must help in the development of workable solutions.

During the first team meeting, all participants must reach a common understanding of the purpose and objectives (goals) of their department, how it functions, and its major problems. A work flow analysis is conducted, systems flow charts can be prepared, and questionnaires are distributed regarding the scope and priority of the principal duties of the department.

As the problems are identified they are given priorities by the team and they are addressed thereby. When the team reaches an agreement as to the basic improvement program to be followed, the details of the solution must be jointly developed by the affected department and the team.

The team should recommend who will responsible for follow-through on each item (usually management.)

Follow-up reports from all team meetings are compiled and forwarded to the owner or manager (depending on the size of the company), who either distributes them for review, revision and additions or actually performs the functions. Any changes, decisions, or comments are relayed back. *This feedback is the key to the program's success.*

Between meetings, team leaders are responsible for follow-up on all items falling under their control and authority. It is also their responsibility to monitor the progress of any follow-up done by their team member.

With participative management, the concept of a supervisor is replaced with that of a group leader who coordinates the work of the employees. In this scenario, a department manager, ultimately responsible for the department's production, coordinates up to five group leaders.

Employees have direct access to the department manager. The group leader is not to act as a go-between. The department acts as an individual company, so to speak, with the manager having total responsibility for setting quotas.

In order for participative management to be effective, employees must understand the concept before it is implemented. *All team members must make a commitment to incorporate the principles of teamwork. And top management must provide the department manager with assistance to define and implement company philosophy; and must provide each group with a team-solving capacity.*

To accomplish the above, management should employ the following procedures:

Team meetings should be held by both department managers and group leaders (vertical teams) and by group leaders and employees (horizontal teams). All work related problems become team problems which the department manager assigns to the vertical or horizontal team best equipped to solve them.

Management coaching sessions should be held regularly (monthly or bi-monthly at the longest.) Under the guidance of a skilled manager or outside consultant, department managers plan the implementation of the goals developed by the individual teams.

Progress meetings should be held monthly to monitor the progress of the teams and encourage the accomplishment of the productivity objectives.

Feedback sessions should be held frequently to reinforce the concept of teamwork.

Any participative team, work team, or consolidated team effort is most effective when the results are recognized with a reward. Incentives, monetary or otherwise, are the ultimate carrot for most employees. The degree or substance of such incentives are management's decision, (possibly a team's), but must be included in the whole framework of the development of employee participation in the future of any company. Specific discussion of the various incentives available requires its own specific study. However, there is should be an incentive for every work situation.

By the use of employee participation teams with incentives, the company's survival is ensured by increased productivity from its human resource. Employee participation teams increase productivity by uncovering problems and developing solutions, while improving employee morale. And a related incentive plan is a strong inducement not only to raise productivity but also to keep it there.

> **McCain's Maxim #12: Follow these tips to improve workplace productivity: (1) Don't over-engineer projects and lose sight of what you're trying to accomplish. Complexity makes productivity improvements hard to achieve. (2) Productivity improvement projects often appear overwhelming. Attack them in bite-size chunks. (3) Include all employees affected by the project, including workers. Teams *may* produce the best results. (4) Be realistic. Blue sky thinking has its place, but only if the idea you conceive is practical and achievable. (5) Track improvements in a timely manner. That way if they aren't producing the improvements you want, it's not too late to change before they damage the bottom line.**

CHAPTER TWELVE

Manage Employee Wages and Wage Expectations

Merit Reviews and Increases Are a Fact of Corporate Life

I recall a conversation I had with a worker in one of my client's manufacturing plants. When I walked by his workstation he asked me if I could stop for a minute and review his scrapbook.

I was curious what his scrapbook contained so I told him I'd be happy to take a look at it. As I watched he flipped through the scrapbook's pages. Every page contained a suggestion he had made resulting in a productivity improvement of his workstation. Each suggestion contained pictures of the improvements along with write-ups by industrial engineers of the money those improvements had generated.

Needless to say I was impressed by the creative suggestions made by the worker, his organizational skills, and that he was proud enough of them to collect a history of his ideas in a scrapbook.

This brought to mind how difficult it sometimes is for managers to motivate employees and how important it is that they reward all of employees for jobs well done. The fact is that wages plus taxes and benefits represent a significant portion of a company's total expenses. It is imperative, therefore, that these expenses be carefully managed and employees duly compensated for their successes.

Basic Concepts about Wages and Employee Wage Expectations

Wage levels and increases are not only two of a

company's most difficult issues, but are controversial among human resource specialists. As such, their treatment here deserves some comments in the way of a foundation.

Employees expect annual wage increases. Do not delude yourself by insisting that no one is guaranteed a raise (which is correct). Not *addressing* this expectation can erode morale. Notice the use of the word *address* Nothing has been said about what should be done since that will vary case by case, but management must understand that ignoring employee expectations is a grave mistake.

Another factor to consider is this: Inflation is pervasive. The influence of real inflation (not the Consumer Price Index; it includes too many factors not impacting the average employee's real spending power) is . . . well, real. In the face of real inflation and no increase in wages, good employees actually experience a reduction in wages. Employees performing satisfactorily have just as much right to expect an increase as the company does in raising its prices.

There probably will be economic times in the life of a company when wage increases are not possible, but that does not change the reality of these statements about employee expectations and inflation.

Do not use the word *raise*. The appropriate term is **merit increase**. No one is entitled to a raise, but everyone should be entitled to a wage which reflects their value to the company, their merit. If real inflation is present, then not providing an adjustment to wages effectively reduces the employee's wages and thereby lowers their merit.

The company can keep wages competitive with the marketplace. Set wages according to what a good employee doing comparable work would be paid in the local marketplace. For instance, an accounts receivable clerk performs work comparable to a bank teller, a position present in all marketplaces and whose comparable wage scale (modified for benefit differences) is usually easy to determine. Failure to maintain competitive wages will eventually erode the overall caliber of company human resources.

Employee performance and earned merit increases are inexorably linked, but you should avoid correlating them in time. *Do not hold discussions with employees concerning performance and a merit review at the same time.* Merit increases are determined by more factors than just performance. Discussing performance and a wage increase at the same time, therefore, does disservice to both issues.

Salary and wages are included in the company's annual budget process, but they are to be managed separately and controlled employee by employee and department by department. This standard procedure will acquaint management with good control mechanisms, so adopting these truths about wages, expectations and inflation should not be alarming. Any wage management program must be administered using carefully designed, objectively oriented procedures. To do otherwise invites allegations of discrimination.

This merit review program fits nicely with incentive programs that reward employees. Wages are included as expenses in arriving at the operating profit which, in turn, has its place in determining incentive levels. If wages are not managed in accordance with the spirit of this merit review program, the employees eligible for the incentives will suffer.

Wage Management and Budget Control

When owners or managers set the annual operating profit goal, they should also consider the *company-wide merit increase factor*. Set a value after considering the following factors: real inflation, the competitiveness of the company's current, overall wage structure, last year's results, and the promise for the future.

Senior management controls the wage management work sheet and completes it just prior to the fiscal year end. It contains all current employees and separates them by department. It also includes each employee's anniversary date. This is their starting date with the company and becomes the day for their annual merit review, an official discussion of their wages.

Once senior management has decided on an appropriate merit increase factor, the department totals should become part of the annual budget.

Procedures for Awarding Merit Increases

The next step in the merit review program is to communicate the merit increase factor to all supervisors. Get their feedback and assure their understanding of its use. They also sign off on the wage budget which results from this. In other words, they agree to hold total wage dollars to the amounts shown in the appropriate right-hand column.

The owner or manager next calls an employee meeting as soon as possible after the fiscal year ends and communicates the company's results. All departments take a few minutes to explain their part in the overall results and congratulate everyone (even if you think it might not be deserved!). *Put a bright face on everything. Be challenging if necessary. Be a leader.*

When a company has not had this type of program in the past, the next step will be for each supervisor to communicate the anniversary date for each employee. This is the date of their annual merit review. *Use employees' starting date as their anniversary date* to assure that increases are staggered throughout the year.

Annually, the owner or manager and his staff will review the following table, which is used to determine employees' merit increase as a percent of their current wages or salaries:

TIME IN CURRENT POSITION

Last Performance Rating*	Under Six Months	Six Months to 1 Yr	One to Two Years	Over Two Years
5	100 percent	110 percent	120 percent	130 percent
4	80 percent	90 percent	100 percent	110 percent

3	70 percent	80 percent	90 percent	100 percent
2	40 -69 percent	None	None	None
1	20 -39 percent	None	None	None

* From 1-5, five being a top rating, one the poorest rating.

How to use this table:

Each employee's merit increase is determined by first finding the correct cell in the above table. Find their last performance rating in the left-hand column (numbered 5 through 1) then follow it over to the percent under the column heading which matches their time in the current position.

Apply the percentage given in that cell to the company-wide merit increase factor *in effect at the time of the merit review.*

For instance, if the employee's last performance rating is a three and they have been in their current position for nine months, the table above shows the company-wide merit increase factor will be adjusted by 80 percent. If the company-wide merit increase factor is six percent, then this employee's merit increase will be six percent times 80 percent, or 4.8 percent of the employee's current wage. This employee will receive a merit increase of 4.8 percent.

This table was constructed on the premise that rewards those with the best performance and longevity in their current position. The table also assumes that those employees new in their current position have already been awarded an increase for expanded responsibilities. If that is not the case, then the department's senior manager can make an exception based upon documented evidence (be wary of potential discrimination). This table also assumes supervisors are following the company's performance appraisal program which typically results in no more than 40 percent of all employees rated excellent five or above average four.

Two weeks before each employee's anniversary date,

their supervisor will call them for a merit review meeting. Supervisors review the latest performance evaluation and time in position and announce a merit increase according to the above schedule (which may be changed by management from time to time). The merit increase is then communicated to the payroll clerk who will make the appropriate adjustment to the paycheck *for the period beginning two weeks after the employee's anniversary date*. Make sure employees are advised of this effective date so they can audit their paycheck and go to their supervisor if there are errors.

Salary Ranges

As the company begins to use this program, they will also need to establish salary ranges for every position in the company.

A salary range is simply a minimum and maximum dollar amount for the position (stated either in terms of an annual salary or an hourly wage). The salary range should be determined after consideration of comparable positions in the company's employment market and the significantly greater value to the company of employees with longevity.

Employees need to know the salary range of their current positions. This will help them understand how they can strive to attain a position of greater responsibilities. It will also show them a point above which they will not receive an annual merit review.

Employees reaching the maximum salary in the range will be informed they are not eligible for annual merit reviews . . . until and unless the company reevaluates that position and increases the salary range. A decision to lower the maximum range in any position may not result in any employee receiving a lower salary. Employees who have reached their maximum salary in the range have reached a plateau.

Periodically, the company reevaluates salary ranges for all positions. Keep these facts in mind:

Salary and wage expenses are a significant portion of the company's total expenses. As such, they must be carefully managed.

The company does not give raises. It awards *merit increases.* Merit increases are awarded when an employee assumes greater responsibility (a promotion) or has achieved performance deserving of reward (the definition of merit).

The company increases salaries and wages by merit reviews and also in accordance with a carefully-designed, objectively-oriented procedure.

Management uses the annual meeting with each employee to discuss the past year's performance and to communicate the upcoming merit increase.

This merit review program effectively integrates budget discipline and employee performance evaluations.

Employee Motivation: Money vs. Non-Monetary Rewards
The basic purpose of motivating employees is to attain increased productivity and/or improved quality of work. Money alone is not a motivator, and in many instances can cause more problems than it solves. Non - monetary means of motivation are often more important than monetary motivation.

Managers and supervisors are responsible for motivating their employees. They do not often have the decision on monetary rewards, but have significant input to the actual decision.

The owner or manager is responsible for the distribution of monetary rewards and/or benefits to subordinates, in accordance with law firm policy and for establishing the limits and basic criteria for distribution of all monetary rewards.

Some of the best motivators for employees are non - monetary and are as follows:

Job Security.

Recognition for effort.

Fair and consistent treatment for all employees.

Honesty.

Being part of a winning team.

Working for a company with a good reputation.

Belief they are among the best at doing their job.

Being faced with new challenges.

Respect for their supervisor.

Input in decisions pertaining to their job.

Belief that they have a chance to grow based on performance.

The type of work they do.

The tools and equipment they work with.

The attitude of their fellow employees.

Difficulty, or ease, of getting back and forth to work.

How society perceives their jobs.

All motivators do not work on all people. It is management's responsibility and job to determine which motivators to use on which employee.

The use of monetary rewards to motivate employees can be in several forms such as cash, time off with pay, overtime, pension plan, health and life insurance. Employees stay with an employer only as long as they perceive their benefits exceed the burden of their job and their motivational needs are met or surpassed.

Non-monetary rewards motivate employees beyond wages. The recognition of effort and achievement is one that most managers need to understand. Managers always seem to find time to tell the employee when they have made a mistake, but often are too busy to express appreciation for a job well done. The recognition needs to be done for a job truly well done, and not just passed around routinely.

The ability to express a personal opinion is generally important to employees, and necessitates management explain why a differing policy (or standard) is adhered to or followed. Management should never feel obligated to justify its every policy or action; explanations to employees should be done within reason.

In return for both monetary and non-monetary rewards, the company has the right to several things from the employee in return for the paychecks and non-monetary rewards they receive including an honest day's work, loyalty, dependability, reliability, honesty, and consistency, and helping the company to teach its goals.

Incentive vs. Bonus

The major difference between an *incentive* and a *bonus* is the knowledge level of the employee as to how the amount is determined. An incentive system is very structured, and the employee can calculate the amount of the incentive owed to him or her, based on defined criteria.

With a bonus program, the employee must realize that the bonus is based on his/her performance, and must also realize that the determination of bonus pay is at the sole discretion of the firm.

One of the problems with an incentive system that says *the company will give you a certain percentage of the net profit* is answering the question, What happens when the estimates were missed, in either direction? If the actual profits are below the amounts estimated the managers and employees work extremely hard just to accomplish breakeven. If the actual profits are above those estimated, employees may receive rewards out of proportion to their individual efforts. This problem can be alleviated or even eliminated by spreading the incentive out over a quarterly period.

Another problem is the need to do a job a second time because it was not performed correctly in the first place, costing the company time and money.

Under a bonus system, the major drawback is that the employee must trust that the determination of distribution is fair. This is why *bonus* programs should be discouraged.

A problem that often occurs in both systems is that the employee begins to believe the bonus is owed to them just for doing his/her normal job, regardless of the profitability of the firm. All bonuses should be paid out of *excess* profits (those which are above projected profits) earned by the company as a direct result of the efforts of a particular function or job. The company has a budgeted profit goal and sales forecast. The profit goal should be attained first, before bonuses are considered.

Management should consider the revenue volume and the profit percentage together. If the revenue volume is exceeded, the profit goals should also be exceeded. If the revenue is down, the profit goal should also be down.

Remember the purpose of an incentive system is to motivate employees and to reward them for performing their job above normal levels, and thus contributing *additional* profits to the company.

Occasionally, the company may encounter windfall types of profit. These are profits due to factors outside of the firm, and are not due to the direct efforts of any function within the firm. These profits should not be shared, but instead used to finance future growth.

In general, money is not the greatest motivator. Motivators in order of importance are:

Sense of achievement.

Earned recognition.

Interest in work itself.

Opportunity for growth.

Opportunity for advancement.

Importance and responsibility.

Peer and group relationships.

Pay.

Fairness.

Company policies and rules.

Status.

Job security.

Friendliness of the supervisor.

Working Conditions.

> **McCain's Maxim #13: One of the most quoted business sayings is A fair day's pay for a fair day's work. This still makes a lot of sense. Owners and**

managers should pay in accordance with performance, and workers should care enough about their jobs to want to do their best. Unfortunately, it doesn't always tend to work that way, but *it is always the responsibility of management to make sure it does.*

CHAPTER THIRTEEN
Install Timely and Cost
Effective Purchasing Procedures

Standardizing Purchasing Procedures Saves Money

The charter for a purchasing department is to assure that parts and materials purchased are of the highest quality and at the lowest possible price from vendors that can be relied upon for on time delivery. The purchasing department is given its budget limits from the owner or manager after consultation with the sales department.

Supply Chain Management

Before examining the traditional role of purchasing. let's take a look at one of the function's newest concepts: supply chain management. In the following discussion. Ross, a supply chain management consultant is explaining the concept to Dave, purchasing manager for a small manufacturer.

"Ross, can you please explain what supply chain management is? All I know about it is that it looks complex."

"Happy to, Dave. Probably the best way to start is with an official definition issued by APICS.[5] Let me read it from their website: 'Supply chain management is the design, planning, execution, control, and monitoring of supply chain activities with the objective of creating net value, building a competitive infrastructure, leveraging worldwide logistics, synchronizing supply with demand and measuring performance globally. '"

"Wow, that's a mouthful."

---

[5] American Production and Inventory Control Society

"Let me express it more clearly. The website Manufacturing ERP has a simplified definition:[6] 'Supply chain management (SCM) is the oversight of materials, information, and finances as they move in a process from supplier to manufacturer to wholesaler to retailer to consumer. Supply chain management involves coordinating and integrating these flows both within and among companies. It is said that the ultimate goal of any effective supply chain management system is to reduce inventory (with the assumption that products are available when needed)'"

"Thanks, Ross. I think I get it now."

"The benefits are more than reduced inventory. If done right it can result in faster movement of goods through the supply chain, lower labor and overhead dollars, and even improve quality."

"I can understand the lower labor and overheard costs, but I don't get the improved quality bit. How does quality relate to supply chain management?"

"Dave, anything that regulates the flow of parts, materials, and information through the entire supply chain can only be accomplished with companies producing high quality products and services. Otherwise the supply chain falls apart."

"Oh, I see it now. In other words since companies have to get the quality part right to use supply chain management, it sort of forces their hand to clean up their quality."

"Dave, you have a way with words. That's exactly right."

"Well, Ross, I can see this working for Wal-Mart, but how about the small to midsized company?"

"Look at it this way. Every company, regardless of size,

---

[6] http://searchmanufacturingerp.techtarget.com/definition/supply-chain-management

can apply some if not all supply chain techniques. They can compress throughput cycles, improve customer delivery promises, use just-in-time to reduce inventory, and reduce scarp and rework. Those are not just the province of larger companies."

"Sounds like a lot can happen to help your company succeed."

"That, Dave, is the bottom line."

In the traditional purchasing system, the purchasing agent will enter purchase orders into the computer at the time purchases are made. All purchase orders will be produced in two copies. Copy one will be kept by the purchasing agent. Copy two will be maintained in the receiving area to be used for receiving of parts and material.

When materials are received the purchasing agent (Or receiving department supervisor) will enter the received materials in the computer then move the purchase order to the accounts payable file for payment of the invoice.

Negotiating Prices and Delivery Dates

The purchasing agent will negotiate prices and delivery dates with vendors. Wherever possible the purchasing department will develop an annual forecast for individual commodities and negotiate prices with vendors based upon anticipated annual purchases. These forecasts may be expressed as average monthly or quarterly usage's and the purchasing agent may commit the company to purchase certain minimal quantities of the materials on a monthly, quarterly or annual basis to assist in the negotiating process with vendors. No purchase orders will be issued to vendors without a corresponding customer demand for that commodity. Any items with annually negotiated prices will be re-bid at the end of each year with all vendors meeting company quality and on time delivery requirements.

For all items purchased on spot buys (no annually negotiated prices) the purchasing agent will seek bids from at least two vendors meeting company quality and on-time delivery requirements every time those items are purchased.

When items are purchased to replenish the raw materials inventory only those quantities of material required to receive the desired quantity discounts will be purchased. It is important that the purchasing agent, working with accounting and inventory control functions, compare the inventory carrying cost with the discounts offered and consider any difficulties associated with ordering or receiving this material prior to ordering replenishment stocks.

The purchasing agent may negotiate with vendors for future delivery dates provided there exists a customer demand for the commodity being purchased. This process will generally be used only when the needed items have a long delivery lead times.

In companies that have multiple locations or deal with on-site customer installations, the purchasing agent will have materials for large jobs delivered directly to the field locations by the vendor. These deliveries to the site location will be at no cost to customers. Deliveries will be made directly to field locations only if there is a company employee on site to accept the delivery.

The purchasing agent will, in concert with the operations or inventory control manager, develop a tracking system for parts and materials purchased. This system should consider quality, proper quantity and on time delivery of all ordered materials by vendor. The tracking system will rate vendors on a 100 point scale with scores of 90 and above indicating vendors we would seek to give more business to as it becomes available and scores below 70 indicating vendors that we wish to replace and give no further business to.

This tracking system will use weighted ratings that will allow the company to assign varying degrees of importance to each of the three criteria being considered when evaluating the vendor.

The purchasing agent will maintain accurate records of all purchases made and all funds spent. All purchases made will be allocated against a customer account and remain within the budgetary limits set by the owner or manager for that account.

The purchasing agent will maintain a vendor file for every vendor used. This file will contain a list of all purchases made from this vendor, any discounts offered by this vendor, materials available through this vendor, the most recent prices paid for material received from this vendor, any problems with late or poor quality material associated with this vendor.

A copy of all purchase orders issued to a vendor will be kept in the vendor file for a minimum of thirty days to assist the purchasing agent in tracking price trends and problems with this vendor. The purchasing agent will determine which vendors to maintain vendor files on based upon the quantity of material purchased, and frequency of use or importance of the vendor to company operations. Purchasing need not keep a vendor file for small or infrequently used vendors.

The purchasing agent will maintain a master purchase order file. This file will contain a complete listing of all purchase orders issued, filed by purchase order number. This file will be broken into active and inactive sections. The active portion of this file will contain all purchase orders issued during the current and previous month. The inactive portion of the file will contain, at a minimum, all purchase orders issued during the past twelve months.   Additional archival files may be maintained at the discretion of the purchasing agent. No open purchase orders may be moved from the active to the inactive files.

The purchasing agent will maintain an open purchase order file in association with the master purchase order file. Any purchase order not filled (as indicated by receipt of a packing slip) on the day of issue will be placed in the open purchase order file. When a packing slip is received, the purchase order will be removed from the open purchase order file and moved to the master purchase order file.

The open purchase order file will be reconciled at least monthly. During the reconciliation process the purchasing agent or another designated company employee will examine all open purchase orders to determine if the materials are still required, or if the items have been received and not reported to purchasing. All items in the open purchase will be canceled if no longer needed, moved to the master purchase order file if received, or followed up with the vendor if not received and still needed.

Once purchase orders have been completed and entered in the computer the purchase order will be sent to the office for payment of the invoice.

The purchasing agent will expedite materials as required to meet job site and shop requirements. Expediting materials to continue or complete a job may include calling for items currently scheduled for future delivery earlier than anticipated, or may require the use of air freight or other forms of expensive transport. If air transport is required the purchasing agent will determine who will pay for the shipment. If the freight is to be paid by the client, the purchasing agent will make whatever arrangements are necessary without further delay. If the freight is to be paid by the company the owner or manager, will inform the purchasing agent to take such actions as are necessary to get the materials to the site or shop location.

Materials will delay or cancel purchase orders when work has not progressed at the anticipated rate and the materials are not needed on the scheduled delivery date. In these cases it is not desirable to have the unneeded materials on site, and the purchasing agent will delay the material deliveries until they are needed. Whenever possible this will be done without expense to the company and without bringing the unwanted material into the shop.

When requests for material are received by the purchasing agent, a check will be made to see if the materials are on hand in the shop prior to ordering the requested materials. If the requested materials are on hand the materials will be issued from existing stocks. Only items not currently in stock will be ordered.

The purchasing agent will, with the concurrence of the owner or manager, establish minimum and maximum stock levels for commonly used materials and supplies. These levels should be set at the lowest possible level to assure that the company has an adequate supply of materials on hand to meet day to day requirements while still meeting any minimum order quantities required by the vendors.

When book levels or physical inventory levels drop below established minimum stock levels the purchasing agent will automatically reorder that material to replenish the inventory to the established maximum level. At the end of the season for the material in question management may wish to delay reorder until a time near the beginning of the next season for that material.

Only commonly used parts and materials will have minimum and maximum stock levels established. All specialty items will be ordered only to meet customer demand.

Monthly and Annual Physical Inventory

The purpose of monthly and annual inventories is to verify the book quantities of parts and materials on hand. It therefore of the utmost importance that both book balances and inventories are maintained and conducted in a timely and accurate manner to assure that the company is not experiencing waste or shrinkage in the inventory.

Monthly physical inventories will be conducted on the last working day of each month under the direction of the operations manager. During the course of the inventory all material and supplies belonging to the company will be counted and recorded for comparison to the book inventory. Small items such as office supplies and minor repair parts will only be counted during the annual inventories in order to expedite monthly inventories.

Once the operations manager, or his designated representative, has completed the physical inventory the results of the inventory will be given to the accounting manager for entry into the computer accounting system.

After entry of the new physical inventory into the computer the accounting manager will compare the current inventory, to the book inventory and develop an inventory variance report for the owner or manager. This report will indicate:

Current stock levels and price of all materials and supplies on hand.

Book stock levels and price of all materials and supplies.

Variance of stock levels from book levels and price.

All inventory sheets will be signed by the person conducting the inventory and turned in to the accounting manager when completed.

> **McCain's Maxim #14: Here are a few tips to successful purchasing: (1) Know your product inside out. (2) Know the sales representatives you deal with and what motivates them. (3) Qualify the sales representatives —who they are and how much leeway they have to negotiate. (4) Know your competitors, their prices, their strengths, and their weaknesses. (5) Buy on price but insist on quality, service, and meeting delivery dates.**

CHAPTER FOURTEEN

Control and Reduce Inventory

For Most Companies Inventory Is Its Most Expensive Cost

In any inventory system, it is important to balance the ordering and carrying costs when selecting quantities to order. There are a number of methods available to achieve that purpose, which are useful and practical.

The major challenge in an active workplace is when and how to use which of the lot sizing methods. ABC Service cannot go into the study and preparation essential to use them in every instance, nor is it necessary. Every stage of inventory control is burdened with the same dilemma: What items to focus control on? Everything cannot be supervised equally.

A relatively universal scale for solving the problem, called inventory turnover ratio, is based on a measure of the return obtained from inventory investments. There is a correlation between turnover ratios that indicates a high percentage of products contribute a low percentage of annual contribution.

The ABC (analysis by contribution) inventory control system is based on the notion of controlling different things differently, so all inventory items are classified by their contribution level and are managed according to that consideration. "A" items are those few that account for 70-80 percent of annual contribution. "C" items are the many items that account for very little, maybe one percent of the annual contribution. "B" items represent the difference in the contributions between "A" and "C".

Management is directed to pay particular attention to "A" items and attempt to keep them turning since they represent the highest return on investment. "C" items justify only simple controls. "B" items merit sound controls, but should require minimal management attention. It is the purpose of this procedure to instruct the user in the practice of ABC analysis.

ABC Analysis

ABC means analysis by contribution, which is the most useful technique for managing inventory by exception. To repeat the supporting Pareto Principle or the 20/80 rule, it says: *In any set of items with different values or contributions, a small fraction of the items contributes a large fraction of the total value of the set."* management by exception, in this case, consists of identifying the few items in the set, to establish strict limits for their control while setting broader limits for the majority of the items representing a small fraction of the total value.

Following is an inventory classification table for a typical inventory spread. This sample indicates that 71.79 percent of the sales dollars for the company came from 5.44 percent of the items. Another 18.21 percent of sales were from another 13.3 percent of the items, and that 10 percent of the sales came from 81.26 percent of the items. This statistical display verifies the Pareto Principle theory that most of the sales dollars came from a few items.

Inventory Classification Table

Classification	Type	percent of Sales	percent of Items
A	**High Volume**	**71.79**	**5.44**
B	**Medium Volume**	**18.21**	**13.30**
C	**Low Volume**	**10.00**	**81.26**
Total		**100.00**	**100.00**

This statistical distribution, called the log-normal distribution, is almost always found in firms' inventories (the degree of concentration of sales among items will vary by company, but the distribution will be similar.) The same distribution will occur within sub-groups. Statistically, graphically, and in a matrix one can see the alignment of ABC inventory status.

Generally the first step in obtaining base data for an analysis of inventory contribution is to identify the company's inventory items and distribute them by value in annual dollars of contribution in descending sequence. This process is regularly performed in operations with a large quantity of inventory items and a computerized system. These systems will also frequently indicate the percentage of sales that each item represents.

You will note that the various levels of volumes have been labeled "A," "B" and "C." In setting inventory policy, items in each of the categories can be given different treatment:

A=fast moving or expensive items
B=medium volume or moderate cost items
C=slow moving or low cost items

The "A" items represent those items which the company does not wish to deplete from its inventory, i.e. minimums must be established to assure that the inventory of "A" items is replenished before the last unit is sold. For "B" items, the company prefers that it does not exhaust the complete supply, but it can survive if an item is occasionally fully sold-out before replacement. For the "C" items, it is often normal to set the minimum at zero unless the item is necessary for use with another item or items with a higher contribution.

There are a number of lot sizing methods available for determining economic quantities for ordering and establishing inventory levels. When using these methods for lot sizing activities, one may determine that only "A" items, which involve the bulk of the volume, will be subject to calculations to determine economic lot sizes. Perhaps "B" items will be lot sized using Fixed Lot (a set quantity ordered when minimums are reached) and "C" using fixed period (a set quantity ordered at pre-set intervals) methods. That way, each class will be given attention at the ordering activity, but only in proportion to its ultimate value to the company. Valuable computer time and management time will not be wasted, only used when it most matters.

In the guidelines set out in lot sizing procedures, there are other considerations when a method is selected. One such is use of more than one lot sizing system. With the onset of computerized systems, this is not as major an issue as it once was, since it is not as difficult to accommodate several types of computations. Yet there is much to be said for a common procedure used for every type of order and all classifications of inventory that doesn't take constant change and result in disruption of a regular work flow.

This procedure was prepared to assist with making selection of lot sizing methods simpler for those responsible. Lot sizing, after all, is the most important part of the inventory management system since it advises management when to buy and how much to buy. There are a number of other situations in inventory management and control that can benefit from focusing on ABC classifications. An example would be physical inventories.

Physical inventory counting by cycle may be structured to give more emphasis to "A" items than to "B" or "C" items. Perhaps "A" items will be counted every month, "B" items every three months and "C" items twice a year. This allows for closer supervision and awareness of what is happening to the more valuable segments of the products. That is what the classification system is meant to do. This allows the company to budget quite exactly for its physical inventory.

While inventory floors (minimums) and ceilings (maximums) are correlated to lot sizing so that all parameters are considered, the initial function of these restrictions is to insure that the dollars tied up in shelf stock are never allowed to exceed budget guidelines. At the same time, there is an insistence that lack of foresight, poor planning or misdirected economy be overridden to the point where a company can be assured of having enough stock to keep its customers served at a predetermined level. A most effective way to judge the allowable expenditures for each product is to use the contribution value of each item and make certain the floors and ceilings are effectively assigned. A company would surely want to count on having more items that produce 20 percent of its sales in safety stock (minimum level) than for an item that produces 0.1 percent of its sales.

Pricing strategies may also be predicated on the ABC method of classification with some additional considerations regarding availability and ease of handling. Of course, competitive conditions must also figure in the tactics. These are sophisticated techniques for assigning markups to these items, but the underlying tenet is to be sure to take what the market will allow based on the viability of the item. There is hardly a better test of viability than contribution to sales.

Likewise, discounts and buying incentives can be offered to customers when they use principally those high volume, high profit items. All of these exercises take careful planning and evaluation of the finalized planned results, but these product variations can provide a good starting point.

Minimum/Maximum Inventory Procedure

Start with the department or product line with the highest inventory value. Identify all items with zero inventories in stock and with no sales within the past one year. After review, delete all of the items identified which are not considered to be standard inventory items. This will reduce the size of the list for future operations.

Next, identify all of those items with in stock quantities greater than zero, which have had no sales within the past year. These items can be considered as "dead" inventory. Review each item and decide whether to keep the item in inventory or to eliminate it from inventory. This is accomplished by:

Selling it at a reduced price (above cost).

Selling it at cost.

Returning it to supplier for a full refund.

Selling it below cost either to other dealers, the general public, or returning to the supplier and paying a restocking fee.

Scrap it or donate it as applicable.

A list must be maintained of the value of all items designated as "dead" inventory to be able to determine if the inventory reduction goal is met. After all departments/product lines have been completed, it may be necessary to reevaluate slow moving items if the desired reduction has not been achieved.

After the "dead" inventory has been identified and disposition determined, establish minimum and maximum levels for the balance of the items. The minimum when entered into the computer system becomes the indication of when to reorder. The maximum level establishes the quantity that is to be ordered when the minimum level is reached. Once established in the computer system, the system can be used to 'flag' when items need to be reordered. The minimum and maximum levels are determined as follows:

What quantity was sold during the past year? What is the average quantity sold per normal delivery period of the item? (If the item turns over frequently, is readily available and is expensive, the minimum quantity may be established as the normal quantity purchased by a customer. If the item is sold once per year or infrequently, the minimum amount may be set as zero.)

What is the normal quantity purchased by the customer?

Will the customer normally wait a day or two for delivery?

What is the delivery time on the item? (Can it be obtained within a day or the same day versus one week or longer?)

What is the value of the item? (If the cost is low and space required is small, consider purchasing the year's requirement on one or two orders to minimize purchasing and handling costs.)

Is it a seasonal item? (When reorder is indicated by the computer system, the purchasing quantity may be reduced or the purchase delayed until the season nears.)

The minimum quantity is established as a result of answering those questions. Setting the maximum levels is determined by answers to the questions shown above plus determining if there a minimum quantity that must be purchased.

If there is a minimum order quantity, the maximum becomes the sum of the minimum desired in inventory plus the minimum that must be ordered. (If the item is inexpensive, ordering by the minimum quantity can be accommodated easily. For more expensive items, consideration must be given to paying more for buying less than the minimum quantity if possible, based on the turnover anticipated during the following year.)

If there is no minimum ordering quantity dictated by the supplier, the maximum level can be determined based upon the normal amount purchased at one time. This number can be modified upwards or downwards depending upon whether it needs to be in inventory and the number purchased normally in a one month period. If an item starts to become "flagged" frequently for reordering, consideration can be given to increasing the maximum level. This procedure is then repeated for each of the departments.

Once established the system becomes self-perpetuating. However, the above steps should be repeated each year for each department as customer buying patterns change and items needed for inventory will change.

Purchases can be made in excess of the order quantity established in the computer system if it is beneficial to obtain quantity discounts; if it is felt that more of an item is needed due to promotions the company plans to run or to cover heavier anticipated purchases during a particular season.

Like all good programs and methods, the ABC inventory control technique is a remarkably useful and multi-purpose plan to aid in exercising management leadership. The ABC theory has been used to establish the minimums and maximums by placing more emphasis on the more expensive items and those that turnover more frequently.

McCain's Maxim # 15: Control and reduce inventory by increasing forecast accuracy, shrink vendor lead time, sell off excess inventory, focus on "A" inventory items, and implement just-in-time inventory techniques.

CHAPTER FIFTEEN

Manage Production Planning and Scheduling

Improve Throughput, Reduce Inventory, and Shrink Lead Times

As the sub-heading above says, managing production planning and scheduling provides many benefits to a company. Without it companies can expect low throughput rates, swollen levels of inventory (itself a company killer), higher labor costs, extended lead times, missed customer promises, excess workers, high overtime, and a host of other ailments that will quickly drive a company into bankruptcy.

Not that the production planning and control process need be complex. In fact, you want it as simple and easy to apply as possible. Read the story at the beginning of Chapter One for a perfect example of the advantages of simplicity.

Definition of Planning and Scheduling Terms

Production unit: An organizational entity responsible for an operational process and having controlled capacity as one of their characteristics.

Production steps: The technological steps of project development: (receipt of material, production, storage, transportation, customer acceptance).

Planning: An activity of managing load and capacity of production units through grounded decision making about accepting new estimates. As the result of proper planning, a balance between production load and production capacity is maintained in relatively long-term perspectives (months ahead).

Scheduling: An activity of managing load and capacity of production units through arranging start and due dates for production steps and assigning employees to certain projects. As the result of proper scheduling, necessary resources are allocated to projects to assure their quality and timely completion in safely manner.

Production load: The amount of work (in man-hours) that is expected to be produced by a production unit in certain time. Production load is determined based on technically grounded estimate.

Production Capacity: The ability of a production unit to produce amount of work in a certain time. When calculating production capacity, management takes into consideration various factors as explained below.

Production Unit Capacity

Capacity of a production unit is determined by:

The number of employees participating in the process (direct labor)

The number of paid work hours during a work day

Labor utilization

Labor efficiency

The labor utilization factor shows a portion of a workday during which an average employee performs work directly related to any job (productive time). Labor utilization factor equals hours worked on direct labor jobs divided by hours paid.

Example: An employee punched in at 6:30 a.m., left at 5:00 p.m., had a 30 minute lunch (unpaid), two 15-minute breaks (paid), idle time of 10 minutes (late from lunch), and spent 20 minutes repairing equipment. His productive time is nine hours, paid time is 10 hours, and labor utilization factor is 90 percent.

There are different (among them legitimate) reasons for non-productive time such as paid breaks and vacations, sick time, inventory and maintenance work, reworks, and idle time. The labor utilization factor cannot be higher than 100 percent.

The planned labor utilization factor is established by the owner or manager to meet budget requirements and is adjusted based on analysis of actual situation.

Actual labor utilization factor is calculated from employee time cards as the ratio between productive time and total time worked (hours paid). The accounting department provides this information weekly. It is the responsibility of each department manager to exceed the planned labor utilization factor.

The labor efficiency factor shows the amount of work produced (in estimated man-hours) by an average employee in a certain amount of productive time. The labor efficiency factor equals to the ratio of work performed (in estimated man-hours) vs. productive time (hours paid).

Among different reasons affecting labor efficiency are such factors as skill and training level, employee morale, existence (or absence) of incentive programs. Labor efficiency factor may be higher as well as lower than 100 percent. Planned labor efficiency factor is established by the owner or manager.

Actual labor efficiency factor is calculated monthly as a ratio between amount of work produced (in estimated man-hours) and productive labor hours occurred during the month. The amount of work produced is provided by the owner's or manager's representative and calculated as equal to the product sold expressed in man-hours + ending work-in-progress inventory − beginning work-in-progress inventory (both also expressed in man-hours).

Example: Work in progress inventory (in estimated man-hours) at the beginning of the month was 200 man-hours, at the end of the month 100 man-hours. Total amount of work released (sold) during the month is 900 man-hours. Amount of work produced equals to 900 + 100 - 200 = 800 man-hours. During the same month employees spent 850 man-hours of productive time (assigned to jobs). Labor efficiency equals 94 percent (800 hours/850 hours =94 percent.)

The Scheduling Process

Work flow through a production process, in order to be efficient and to maximize productivity, must be tightly scheduled and controlled. Otherwise, either work does not get into the production pipeline or slack or unproductive time develops within the process. Either condition may increase costs to the detriment of profits and customer satisfaction—which also affects profits in the long term.

Tools are available that allow managers to effectively schedule work flow in order to maximize productivity and to minimize excess costs. The schedule board is central to having an efficient system because it highlights the jobs that stand in line, both in the process and waiting to enter the process. Logical application of associated planning methods allows managers and schedulers to move jobs through the process in the best order practicable.

This procedure discusses creating the schedule and the associated methods that can be used to regulate and improve production flow.

The first step in creating a well-managed production flow is to chart the jobs in a format that allows managers, schedulers, and workers to readily view the jobs in process and waiting to enter the shop. The format must clearly identify the individual jobs; the critical times tied to each job—e.g., date in, date promised, and actual date delivered; the work required to be completed; and the status of the job through the flow.

The form of the chart may be in a computer, written on paper, or displayed on a large board. Whatever the format, the essential information must be entered and tracked by the flow managers. When first setting up the system, several trial runs may be necessary to determine which information is essential to

the flow's control, and additional changes to the format likely
will be necessary over time in order to keep up with changes in
the production system.

The schedule board and the information contained on it
must be readily available to every employee who works within
or who has an impact on the flow process in order that the
system may be most beneficial to the company.

Job Scheduling

Each job must be entered on the schedule according to a
logical and consistent pattern: e.g., date in, date due out, size of
job, contents of job.

The scheduler must be aware of factors that affect the
cost of the job, such as the date when a penalty will take effect,
the date when the company becomes liable for providing
replacement services, the date or time when certain support
services are or are not available, or the availability of production
resources—workers, work space, parts, and materials.

The selection of jobs to enter production must be made
using rational criteria that include the description of work, the
amount of work, the availability of workspace, the expertise of
the employees, and the number of jobs still to enter production.

Certain jobs may be assigned a higher priority due to
factors external to the selection criteria. Customer influence,
insurance demands, and similar factors may influence
scheduling.

The scheduler may establish policy regarding the
priority of jobs to be selected. It should be noted that always
selecting large jobs over small jobs, or the reverse, normally
will result in an imbalance in the type of job waiting to enter
production. Most processes cannot effectively absorb both kinds
of jobs in that kind of sequence without accumulating a large
backorder list of the unselected job type. Therefore, a rational
mix of jobs must be selected for processing so that a typical mix
of waiting jobs remains.

Although complex statistical formulae have been developed to assign priorities to jobs, probably the easiest method for job selection is to determine the ratio of small jobs to large jobs and select new jobs according to that ratio. For example, if the number of small jobs equals 15 at three days each, while the number of large jobs equals five at fifteen days each, the scheduler may select either three small jobs for every large job based on the number of jobs (15:5 = 3:1);

Whenever a large job is entered into the production flow, that job must not be unnecessarily delayed in reaching completion. To have a job sitting in a bay without work being done reduces overall bay productivity and increases cost per bay which, in turn, reduces the gross margin of that particular job, and reduces profitability of the entire operation.

Very small jobs may be entered into the production flow when those jobs do not take up real production space and when they may be worked in to the slack time inherent in any job set. These small jobs generally contribute to overhead and profit when the actual space and time consumed is minimal relative to the overall process allocation.

The scheduler retains the right to make day-to-day judgments on which unit enters the production process. Alternative scheduling systems may be superimposed upon the master scheduling system. For example, the scheduler may choose to run one subset of units during one day or week, changing to another subset the following day or week. This method allows the scheduler to maintain the balance of small to large while ensuring that certain obligations are being met.

Effective production scheduling is necessary to maximize gross margin, minimize the list of backorder jobs, and maintain customer satisfaction. The system must be easily understood by those who work within the system or whose work is impacted by the system.

Scheduling is a dynamic process, subject to change on a daily or even hourly basis. Even so, scheduling is critical to maintaining an effective production flow, and it must be implemented with discipline and with full awareness of the changing mix and demands of the jobs on hand.

Production Scheduling Procedure for a Gun Manufacturer

What follows is a procedure used to outline the process of planning and scheduling production for a gun manufacturer.

The basic function of production planning and scheduling is to provide a framework for expediting the completion of customer orders, while producing those orders with a minimum of expense.

A work order will be made out for each gun on a sales order. Blank work orders are numbered in sequence and should be located in one place. This will be at the scheduling desk. A picking slip will be made out for all items on the sales order not manufactured.

The work orders for each sales order will be listed on the gun production schedule, and the sales department notified as to the week when the sales order is scheduled to be shipped.

Each gun production schedule should be for one week's output, or a group of scheduling forms that make up one week's output.

The scheduling supervisor takes the gun production schedule for the week and groups the guns by caliber. Lists the specialty items to be manufactured and the different type of grips on the week's schedule.

Production Control will develop a daily schedule of guns to be assembled for two weeks ahead. Each Thursday morning the assembly and buffing foreman should assign a person to assemble each gun on the two weeks of scheduling. The next week's schedule should be approved by the production manager. The picking slip is sent to shipping and all items pulled and placed in staging for that sales order.

Production Control should give to the storeroom supervisor a schedule for two weeks of assembly. The parts needed to assemble all the guns and accessory parts would be placed on a cart for each week's schedule.

Each Friday the cart with the parts for next week's guns to be assembled should be sent to the assembly area. The second cart with one week's parts should remain in staging. The parts for one more week should be pulled and placed on a cart and put in staging. (There should be one cart in assembly area, one cart for the next week in staging and one cart with parts for third week being pulled and placed in staging) As each cart with one week's parts goes to assembly area, another week's parts will be pulled and placed on a cart in staging.

Each week a parts shortage list should be compiled. This list should be checked with the back-log of guns to insure that there will be enough parts to build the guns scheduled.

Each part in the inventory should have a maximum and a minimum quantity. Issue a work order to build enough parts to bring the quantity to the maximum amount.

The work orders for the parts are scheduled by Production Control to meet the weekly schedule. All sub-assemblies are scheduled to meet the final assembly schedule.

Production Control should submit a requisition to purchasing for the material needed and give them a schedule as to delivery dates.

McCain's Maxim #16: When managing production planning and scheduling, keep in mind that the accuracy of inventory numbers, routings, bills-of-materials, and lead times are critical, whether you are working with a computerized system such as MRP or with a manual system. And don't forget to build in contingency time in the system to handle the unexpected.

CHAPTER SIXTEEN

Cut Rejects and Improve Customer Satisfaction Through ISO Standards of Quality Management

High Quality Is the Core Ingredient of a Successful Company

The quality management system described below is based on a manufacturing company—call it OPQ, Inc[7].—with a documented quality management system designed and implemented to fulfill ISO 9001 requirements. This system creates a framework for clearly defining the control of materials, processes and inspection activities. In turn, our customers are assured that OPQ, Inc. service is provided in a well-defined and controlled environment.

All employees who manage, perform or verify work affecting quality are responsible for implementing the quality system. The quality management representative is responsible for coordinating, monitoring and auditing the system. Implementation of the quality system is assessed regularly by way of internal and external audits and management reviews.

Quality Planning

Quality plans assure that the following items are understood and considered:

All functional areas identify the processes, controls, equipment, resources and skills needed to meet the required quality.

---

[7] A fictitious company

Procedures, as applicable, are in place for all the processes to meet the quality requirements.

The latest applicable technology is being used to assure OPQ, Inc. remains competitive with its competitors.

Standards for quality and performance are checked to determine their applicability and acceptability in meeting the requirements.

Contract Review

The goal of contract (order) review is to confirm the agreement to customer orders prior to acceptance and the resolution of any differences, and capabilities of the company to meet customer requirements.

OPQ, Inc. assures that all customer requirements can, in fact, be met without any nonconformance. Contracts (orders) will be reviewed to assure that the requirements are adequately defined and documented. Where no written statement of requirement is available for a contract (order) received by verbal means, the person receiving an order shall assure that the contract (order) requirements are agreed before their acceptance. The company will resolve differences between accepted order requirements and those in the contract are resolved, and that OPQ, Inc. has the capability to meet the accepted contract or order requirements.

While amendments are a fact of life in companies which strive toward top-notch customer service as OPQ, Inc. does, they will not cause the disruption to the company business that is commonly seen in companies of lesser quality orientation. Every effort will be made to honor customer contract amendments that are within our ability to meet their requirements.

An amendment to a contract (order) includes but will not be limited to changes in delivery times, project change of scope, financial arrangements, quantity, cancellation of the service altogether.

Document and Data Control

OPQ, Inc. quality system documentation comprises the following types of documents: quality manual, standard procedures, standards and other reference material, and quality plans.

All appropriate documents are readily available at all areas where operations essential to the quality system take place.

All documents are reviewed and approved prior to issue. Documents are distributed to employees and locations where they are used. Any changes in a document are detailed, reviewed, and approved by the relevant people prior to issue. Revised portions of documents are distributed with a change brief and obsolete documents are promptly removed by the issuing employees.

Purchasing

This section of the standard is applicable to parts and materials bought by OPQ, Inc. for goods to be incorporated into designed, assembled, and installed products. The information provided on the purchase order is adequate to specify the requirements of the order.

Methods of verification purchased products by OPQ, Inc. or by its customers at the subcontractor's premises are specified in the purchasing documents, as necessary.

Product Identification and Traceability

OPQ, Inc. assures that products maintain identification and traceability during all stages of delivery, when required by the customer or a governing regulatory agency or when OPQ, Inc. determines that the practice would be prudent.

Process Control

Key processes that directly affect quality of OPQ, Inc. products include project scheduling, manufacturing, and assembly, (where the latter two have unchallenged priority) are subject to process control to assure that they are carried out under controlled conditions.

Project Scheduling is performed by the representatives of the owners or managers with the purposes of ensuring timely completion of every accepted order. Project Scheduling implementation and follow-up is controlled in the course of regular (weekly, daily) management and/or sectional meetings. Minutes of the meetings are filed by the owner or manager, as applicable.

Manufacturing and assembly are carried out by trained and qualified employees only. Qualification of each newly hired employee is checked against the job description to insure adequacy of his/her experience and training. Performance of each employee is evaluated on continuous basis (one of the evaluation criteria is workmanship). Workmanship requirements are spelled out in design documentation and (as necessary) in special work instructions and/or in representative samples. Employees who do not measure up to the workmanship criteria are counseled on how to improve and meet OPQ, Inc. workmanship requirements. The owner or manager determines the necessity of developing work instructions and/or samples.

Assembly and inventory areas and equipment are maintained regularly to provide a suitable working environment. All processes and methods used by OPQ, Inc. employees are in full compliance with reference standards/codes and federal and state regulations. All equipment is regularly maintained following the schedules and recommendations provided by their manufacturers.

Process work instructions and/or samples and equipment used are approved by owner or manager or their representatives as applicable.

Conditions, under which key processes are carried out, are checked regularly by managers of the company or by a designated employee.

Inspection and Testing

In order to verify that the specified requirements are met, OPQ, Inc. performs receiving, in-process, and final inspections and testing of its products. The company keeps records to show all inspection and test results.

OPQ, Inc. employees inspect received parts and material used for various components of equipment to assure that they meet specifications and purchase order requirements. In deciding the amount of incoming inspection/testing that is required, past performance of the supplier as well as any knowledge in regard to the amount of quality control exercised by the supplier at their premises are considered. OPQ, Inc. prefers to use ISO certified suppliers.

In-process and final inspection and testing are regulated by design documentation and, as necessary, special work instructions. The owner or manager determines the necessity of developing special work instructions. They are to be approved by owner or manager, as applicable.

As OPQ, Inc. finished products are designed and built on conceptual applications, no equipment is delivered until all components have been subjected to final testing to assure compliance with a customer's application. Only equipment that passes the final inspection is allowed to be delivered and installed on a customer's property. In completing the documentation segment of the process, the amount and type of product delivered will be double-checked prior to delivery.

Records of all inspection activities are maintained for a minimum period of three years after delivery completion. Test equipment and test records are indicative of all of the results against stated designed requirements and indicate the results attained.

Equipment with correct calibration settings that are traceable to industry standards is provided for the purpose of identification and inspection on product quantity, distances traveled, and equipment condition, to cite examples.

The measuring and test equipment that requires calibration is identified in ISO 9001 as *Control of Test Equipment.* This standard procedure also includes the calibration schedule and the control procedures to be followed that comply with requirements of ISO 9001.

All equipment used for testing and measuring and their calibration status is subject to unique identification with stickers attached. Records of calibration are maintained and a recall system established. When equipment is found to be out of calibration, the effect of that error on prior services will be reviewed and appropriate corrective action taken.

It is the responsibility of all assigned operating employees to assure that the equipment used is suitable and within its calibration period.

To assure that only product that has passed the required inspections and tests is dispatched, used, or installed, OPQ, Inc. identifies inspection and test status of inspected and tested materials, parts, assemblies, and equipment. The identification includes different methods such as marking, tagging, and/or location, as applicable.

Control of Non-conforming Product

OPQ, Inc. uses testing and inspection to determine products, parts and material conformance to customer requirements (for example, specifications and regulations). Whenever a product, a part, or a material either through inspection or a suspect process is considered nonconforming (regardless of how insignificant non-conformities seem to be or how easily they can be repaired), it is identified, documented, evaluated, segregated, and disposed. Functions concerned are informed about relevant activities regards to each case of nonconformity.

OPQ, Inc. uses the following methods of disposition:

Rework: Action taken in nonconforming product so it will meet the specific requirements.

Repair or Use As Is: Action taken on nonconforming product so that the product will fulfill the intended usage although the product may not conform to the original requirements or specifications. Decisions to accept nonconforming product without rework must be concurred upon in writing by the customer.

Scrap.

Return to Supplier.

For nonconforming product (equipment) that is to be repaired or reworked, instructions will be prepared, reviewed and approved in the same manner as the original work instructions. Reworked products are re-inspected in accordance with the appropriate inspection procedure.

Corrective and Preventive Action

OPQ, Inc. recognizes that diligent and effective implementation of the corrective action policy is crucial to the success of the quality system. OPQ, Inc. has documented procedures for implementing corrective and preventive actions to identify root causes and possible problems, or deficiencies in the company quality system and to determine what improvements and changes might be needed in the quality system. This information is also used to determine product quality and to demonstrate the effectiveness of OPQ, Inc.'s quality system.

The corrective and preventive action procedures specify a structured problem solving method that is used to resolve problems in quality, productivity and other performance areas.

Applications of corrective action include handling complaints, reports on product problems, investigating causes and documenting the results, determining corrective action required, and installing the proper controls to assure that effective actions are executed.

Applications of preventive action include using information sources to locate, review and eliminate problem causes, the identification of action plans focused on preventive action, the implementation of effective controls, and timely and accurate communication on preventive actions taken with management.

Revisions to documented procedures as a result of corrective and preventive actions are recorded and implemented. This policy applies to both internal and external problems and/or concerns. This procedure includes (1) effective handling of customer complaints and reports of problems., (2) investigating the causes of nonconformities and recording results of the investigation, (3) determination of the corrective actions needed to eliminate the cause of nonconformities, and (4) verification that corrective actions are taken and are effective, (5) maintaining and utilizing information on performance to detect, analyze and eliminate potential causes of nonconformities, (6) planning the steps needed to resolve problems discovered, management review and approval, obtaining customer approval where needed, executing the plan and verifying the results, (7) implementation and recording of changes in procedures resulting from preventive actions.

Handling, Storage, Packaging, Preservation, and Delivery

All products and materials are handled, stored and transferred throughout the process from product receiving to inventory and on into the assembly process in such a manner as to prevent damage or deterioration.

Special methods of handling, storage, packaging, preservation, and delivery of OPQ, Inc. products are prescribed by design documentation and/or special work instructions. The necessity of developing work instructions is determined by the owner or manager. Work Instructions are approved by any of the shop foreman, as applicable. The shop foreman is responsible for maintaining the system for handling, storage, and delivery of products by OPQ, Inc.

Appropriate general methods for handling, storage, packaging, and preservation, (when the materials, parts, and products are controlled by OPQ, Inc.) and for delivery (while in transit to destination) are in place at OPQ, Inc. to assure conformity of products delivered to customers. Delivery to customers is arranged for by our customers and performed by common carrier and/or customer designated means.

Control of Quality Records

Quality records provide the evidence that the quality management system is operated in accordance with documented procedures and that it is effective. OPQ, Inc. has documented procedures for control of the quality records. The accuracy of the quality records is analyzed every time they are reviewed for the purpose of developing corrective and preventive action.

Quality records are stored for quick and easy retrieval, and protection from loss, damage or deterioration. A written record retention program exists including destruction of the records at the expiration period. The quality records are available for customer evaluation if required, and are retained in accordance with customer and regulatory agency requirements.

Records are usually established by the employees directly involved with the task, operation, or activity which results need to be recorded. Records identify the product, person or event to which they pertain; they provide the relevant facts and data and are signed and dated by the person who established the record.

Specific record formats are usually prescribed by the procedures that call for their establishment. These can be forms, reports, minutes of meetings, stamps placed on other documents, or other. Records can also be established and maintained on computer files and databases.

Records are indexed and grouped to facilitate their retrieval. Binders, drawers, and cabinets containing records are clearly labeled with identification of their contents. Records may not be stored in private desk drawers or other obscure locations that are not generally known.

Internal Quality Audits

OPQ, Inc. has documented procedures for conducting internal quality audits in compliance with the requirements of ISO 9001.

The purpose of the internal quality audits is to confirm quality system conformance, identify areas requiring corrective action, and to test the effectiveness of the quality system. The internal audits assure that we are doing what our documented quality system says we are doing.

All audits are regularly conducted by auditors having an independent relationship to the audit target areas. The auditors have been trained through an internal quality auditor training program.

Selected activities are audited more frequently, depending on their importance and quality performance history. The audit schedules remain dynamic responding to the health of the quality system.

Audit reports are an agenda item for discussion at the quality management review. Appropriate follow-up actions are organized to assure effective audits.

Training

All functions within the company which might be affected by the lack of acquired skill and training are identified and made the subject of job descriptions which reflect the extent and evidence of skill and training required. These will be used to appraise the level of competence of employees both during probationary or training periods and on an ongoing basis to assure continuing education and training needs.

All staff receives appropriate training before carrying out assigned functions and responsibilities. On-the-job training programs are prepared to assure complete familiarity with all requirements of the company. Records are maintained on training given and completion of training is subject to an end-of-training review. Periodic reviews of training requirements are made to assure that training remains effective and to identify needs for re-training and cross-training.

All managers are responsible for ensuring that only employees who are fully qualified perform tasks requiring specific skills.

McCain's Maxim # 17: Too many owners and managers consider quality a technical methodology

and as such delegate it to the quality department. But high quality is only capable when every employee, from top to bottom, considers it his or her responsibility. The technical part is important, of course, but even more so is the attitude that everybody must pitch in to make it happen.

CHAPTER SEVENTEEN

Install a Responsive Human Resources Function

Make HR Responsible for Keeping Its
Fingers on the Pulse of Employee Morale

The human resources (HR) director of a company told me this story:

I had just been hired as HR director for the job I held now when our department was charged with the responsibility for hiring our new vice president of marketing. In the course of conducting interviews we narrowed the selection to four candidates. Of the four candidates one had outstanding credentials and exactly the industry experience we were seeking.

This candidate's name was Hastings Benson Goodwin[8], a blueblood from New England with the right educational background: Phillips Academy, then on to Yale where he graduated summa cum laude. He worked for a large conglomerate called TGE[9], progressing rapidly through the ranks, to product manager for one of the company's major businesses.

This was precisely the type of job candidate our chief executive was seeking, because he had a similar background. I'm sure you know how that goes. What the top guy wants the top guy gets.

But I was not as sure about hiring Goodwin. He didn't fit the profile of our company. Our employees, including most of the

---

[8] Fictitious name

[9] Fictitious name

executive staff (except our CEO) were the rough hewn type, most of them without impressive educational credentials, the type who started at the bottom and clawed their way to the top. TGE, by contrast, was a gentleman's club, with a preponderance of executives with prep school and Ivy League backgrounds.

Still, Goodwin impressed the executives at our company. He gave the impression of being an ordinary guy, and won over the managers and executives who interviewed him.

But . . . there was something about him, some elusive quality that aroused my suspicions. I couldn't quite put my finger on it but the feeling lingered after Goodwin's interview and I knew I had to put it to rest.

I checked his references; every one gave Goodwin outstanding praise. Frankly, that also made me suspicious. I've been in this business twenty-five years and it's seldom that I come across such unalloyed tribute. Was this guy Goodwin a miracle worker?

Turns out he wasn't. I hired an investigator to check on Goodwin's background and what I discovered both shocked and amazed me. Hastings Benson Goodwin, Yale graduate, was real, but it wasn't the same Hastings Benson Goodwin that interviewed with my company.

The guy's real name was Mike Kowalczyk, from the south side of Chicago. Mike never graduated from Yale, never even attended there. After high school he spent eight years in the Marine Corps, and then worked for a succession of small companies in and around Chicago before deciding he wanted something better. He searched the Internet and found the name of somebody from Yale who graduated the same year Mike left the Marine Corps, **then legally changed his name to Hastings Benson Goodwin.** *From there he fabricated his background and paid off a couple of cronies to act as references, and we almost bought it.*

Needless to say, we didn't hire Mike. But the point of the story is that had we done so, and had Mike's real background emerged over the years as surely it would have, my department and the executive team at our company would have been made a laughing stock among our employees and the community. And that kind of fiasco brings down employee morale because nobody likes working for dunces. One thing I learned early in my career is that employee morale is critical to the success of a company and it's delicate enough to handle it with deliberation and empathy.

Here's a story of my own: In one of the companies I consulted with, Leo was sort of looked down upon by his boss, the HR manager. Leo, whose background included several years as a shop floor worker, and later as a union shop steward, had been promoted to a salaried position as employee relations specialist. One of the main aspects of his job as Leo saw, involved staying on top of the latest rumors floating around on the plant grapevine. His boss didn't agree. He wanted Leo to spend his time involved with administering the employee performance review program and other related tasks such as preparing job descriptions.

But Leo knew the workers well and understood that trouble often brews beneath the surface while managers and supervisors are unaware of storm clouds approaching.

Leo had been hearing rumors lately of a possible walkout if the company didn't resolve an outstanding problem regarding how overtime was distributed among workers. When Leo brought this problem to his boss, the HR manager, he dismissed Leo's concerns and told him to stop paying attention to rumors.

But the plant manager was savvy and had regularly used Leo to tap the concerns of the plant's workers. He listened to Leo's opinion of the latest chatter and raised hell with the HR manager until HR modified the overtime rules in time to avoid a strike. Thanks to Leo a walkout was averted.

Morale among employees is one of the key charter responsibilities for professional HR executives and managers. Sure, HR is also responsible for administering benefits, labor contract negotiations, preparation of employee hand books and job descriptions, and other related duties, but its chief duty is keeping its pulse on the organization and making sure it advises senior management when it detects a brewing morale problem.

In line with this thinking, the following sections describe three representative HR jobs that are key to maintaining high employee morale.

Employee Relations

Managing employee relations is crucial to managing a successful company. This section describes key elements in a successful employee relations function.

Employee relations is responsible for performing various employee relations duties, including counseling with employees, promoting equal employment opportunities, implementing disability accommodations, participating in new employee orientation, advising managers on employees actions, and resolving employee complaints. Assists management in developing and implementing effective employee relations policies and procedures. Keeps management informed of area activities. Assists employees as needed.

Essential Functions and Basic Duties

Assumes responsibility for developing and effectively implementing employee relations policies.
Assures employees are treated fairly and consistently according to established company policies and procedures and legal regulations.

Advises managers of established procedures relating to employee relations issues.

Participates in educating and training company employees regarding employee relations principles and practices.

Makes recommendations to management in the development and revision of employee relations policies.

Assumes responsibility for the effective performance of employee relations functions.

Counsels with employees to resolve complaints involving working conditions, harassment, disciplinary actions, and related matters. Recommends solutions according to company policies and procedures and applicable legal requirements.

Works with managers to assure equal opportunities are provided to all employees. Provides counsel on employee situations and recommends disciplinary actions if appropriate.

Develops and implements programs and services for disabled workers. Assures fair treatment.

Participates in new employee orientation, educating employees on equal employment principles.

Assumes responsibility for establishing and maintaining effective communication, coordination, and working relations with company employees and management.

Aids and supports supervisors and managers in handling employee relations matters.

Coordinates functions with other departments. Provides support as required.

Keeps management informed of area activities and of any significant problems.

Completes related reports and documents promptly and accurately.

Assumes responsibility for maintaining professional business relations with government officials and trade professionals.

Serves as a liaison between the company and government officials and business contacts.

Assures the company's professional reputation is maintained.

Assures questions and concerns are promptly and courteously resolved. (The importance of this should not be underestimated. When employee's concerns are not responded to, morale drops faster than a cement block off the back of a pickup truck.)

Assumes responsibility for related duties as required or assigned.

Stays informed of trends and changes in the human resources field.

Performance Measurements
Employee actions are handled fairly, consistently, and in compliance with legal requirements and company policies.

Complaints are resolved without legal action.

Managers and employees are well-informed of employee relations policies and procedures.

Appropriate guidance and counsel is given to managers and employees alike.

Programs and services for disabled workers are effectively developed and implemented.

Issues relating to separating employees, such as exit interviews and unemployment claims are handled consistently and fairly.

Assures that effective communication and coordination exists with company departments. Assistance is provided as needed.

Labor Relations
Managing labor relations is crucial to managing a successful company. This section describes key elements in a successful labor relations program with emphasis on the union.

Labor relations is responsible for overseeing and administering labor relations functions including negotiations, hiring practices, promotions, terminations, and wage policies. Assures all employee and labor actions are resolved in a fair, consistent, and legal way.

Builds and maintains effective relations with unions, union officials, and government agencies.

Negotiates labor contracts with labor unions.

Consistently enforces company labor policies and procedures, and legal regulations.

Resolves grievances.

Assures supervisors and managers receive adequate training on labor relations procedures.

Essential Functions and Basic Duties
Assumes responsibility for the development and implementation of effective labor relations planning and establishment of policies.

Assists senior management with long and short term labor relations planning. Develops a total strategy and direction for the company's labor relations functions.

Executes established goals and assures labor policies support and complement company strategies and goals.

Develops and implements union contract negotiation strategies which further company objectives. Assists Senior management in developing related budgets.

Continually evaluates established policies and procedures and updates or modifies them as necessary.

Assumes responsibility for the effective management of labor relations.

Administers and interprets provisions of all labor agreements in force.

Manages all contract negotiations with labor unions, including issues relating to grievances, salaries, benefits, and employee welfare.

Acts as liaison between company management and union representatives to assure problems are resolved.

Assures the company is in compliance with all labor agreement provisions.

Works to continually improve labor relations.

Assumes responsibility for effective management of all labor relations functions.

Recommends and directs wage/labor polices based on union requirements and objective data regarding competition, profitability, business conditions, and the economic environment.

Oversees the education of company employees and Managers on labor relations issues.

Works to resolve labor complaints involving working conditions, harassment, and disciplinary actions.

Recommends actions to resolve labor complaints according to company policies and applicable legal requirements.

Advises managers on employee actions including hiring, promotions, and terminations. Recommends disciplinary action if appropriate. Assures compliance with established company policies, union contracts, and applicable legal requirements.

Conducts exit interviews with separating employee to gain perspective on company policies and employment practices. Discusses exit interview findings with management as necessary.

Responds to and follows through on all unemployment claims the company attempts to deny.

Oversees and assures the consistent, fair, and legal application of labor relations functions.

Effectively supervises labor relations employee, ensuring optimal performance.

Provides leadership to staff through effective objective setting, delegation, and communication. Conducts staff meetings as required.

Assures staff is well trained, effective, and optimally used. Instructs staff regularly regarding policy, procedure, and program changes.

Conducts performance appraisals as required. Formulates and implements corrective actions as needed.

Assures staffing levels are appropriate.

Assumes responsibility for establishing and maintaining effective communication, coordination, and working relations with company employee and management.

Aids and advises supervisors and department managers in handling labor matters such as hiring, promotions, and disciplinary actions.

Keeps management informed of area activities and of any significant problems.

Assumes responsibility for maintaining professional business relations with labor unions and trade professionals.

Serves as a liaison between the company and government officials, labor leaders, and business contacts.

Represents the company with various trade professionals and groups.

Assures the company's professional reputation is maintained.

Assures questions, concerns, and grievances are promptly and courteously resolved. (The importance of this should not be underestimated. When employee's concerns are not responded to, morale drops faster than a cement block off the back of a pickup truck.)

Stays informed of trends and changes in the union environment and human resources field.

Performance Measurements
Assures that contract negotiations are handled legally and appropriately.

Assures that relations with labor unions are professional and productive.

Assures that labor actions are handled fairly and in compliance with legal requirements and company policies.

Assures that effective labor policies are established, communicated, and implemented.

Assures that department employees are well trained, effective, and efficient. Appropriate supervision and assistance are provided. Company employee are well-educated on labor relations policies.

Assures that effective communication and coordination exist with company departments. Assistance is provided as needed.

Assures that management is appropriately informed of area activities and of any significant problems.

Assures that effective business relations exist with governmental, trade, and business professionals.

Training

Effective employee training is an essential component of employee morale. Employees well trained to handle their jobs are employees without stress related to job performance. This section describes key elements in a successful training function.

The training coordinator is responsible for coordinating all aspects of the master employee training schedule.

Compiles training information, creates and distributes schedules, and assures they are accurate, complete, and free from errors.

Responsible for coordinating facilities, materials, computer equipment, and refreshment arrangements for training classes.

Handles student enrollment, class registration, and student records functions.

Assures records are efficiently and accurately maintained. Effectively communicates with outside contacts and company employee.

Essential Functions and Basic Duties
Assumes responsibility for coordinating the assembly and distribution of the master employee training schedule.

Assembles, prints, and distributes master employee training calendar.

Assures training schedule is accurate and complete, with a variety of dates and times offered for each subject.

Writes and includes course descriptions in training schedule.

Makes arrangements for trainers of each subject.

Incorporates input from managers on training needs and requirements.

Assumes responsibility for coordinating facility arrangements for training classes.

Assures training rooms are clean, in good repair, and maintained at a comfortable temperature. Handles complaints professionally.

Assures computers, monitors, and projection equipment are appropriately set up and ready prior to class.

Assures printed support materials are well correlated to course topics.

Assures an adequate number of tables, chairs, and student materials for class.

Efficiently handles and coordinates student enrollment and records functions.

Collects and maintains student registration information. Assures proper class size.

Collects fees and forwards to appropriate accounting employee.

Provides accurate class information including date, time, address, and travel and parking directions.

Distributes class information to enrolled students in advance of class.

Maintains records of student test scores if applicable.

Communicates scores to managers as appropriate.

Assumes responsibility for ensuring professional business relations exist with facility management, vendors, travel providers, and trade professionals.

Represents the company in contacts with equipment and food vendors, travel professionals, equipment repair employee, and trade professionals.

Assures requests, questions, and problems are courteously and professionally resolved. Assures communications are efficient and effective.

Assures the company's professional reputation is maintained both internally and externally.

Assumes responsibility for establishing and maintaining effective communication and coordination with company employee and management.

Assists and supports related departments as required.

Keeps management informed of area activities and of any significant concerns.

Stays informed of new training developments.

Assures departmental work areas are clean, secure, and well maintained.

Completes special projects as assigned.

Performance Measurements
Assures that the master employee training schedule is effectively coordinated, printed, and distributed.

Assures that the training courses offered support the goals, objectives, and requirements of management.

Assures that the training facility details and arrangements are appropriately made. Computer equipment is set up appropriately. Training materials, arrangements, and fees are cost effective and meet budget constraints.

Assures that student enrollment is efficiently and professionally coordinated. Class sizes are appropriate.

Assures that student records and test scores are carefully maintained and communicated.

Assures that good relationships exist with outside service providers.

Assures that management is appropriately informed of training activities.

McCain's Maxim #18: Keeping in touch with employees on the firing line can head off developing problems. In one case an HR specialist in an auto company alerted management to a possible walkout over an issue management considered insignificant. Company executives adroitly changed course and their recognition of the problem and subsequent actions avoid the walkout.

CHAPTER EIGHTEEN

Penetrate Markets and Raise Sales Levels

An Effective Marketing and Sales Plan
Is Key to Company Success

Let's examine a case study: QRS, a welding supply company, is in a very competitive industry. Several opportunities are available for expansion; however, due to limited capital available for expansion, the company must focus on the most viable option. To determine the best course of direction, management must objectively weigh all alternatives and their risk-reward potential.

Once an expansion and market opportunity is identified, information must be gathered to determine each opportunity's criteria that management should review before embarking on any expansions.

Marketing Analysis

There are two types of expansion opportunities: (1) within existing markets, such as expanding sales and marketing efforts in the welding equipment, supplies and industrial gas sales, and (2) penetrating a new market segment. The marketing analysis remains the same for either expansion type. Listed below are the criteria used in analyzing and comparing the available options.

Competition. How competitive is the market and how strong are the competitors? Competitor information is available from sources such as potential customers, competition, employees, and competitor's employees. What are their strengths and weaknesses? How difficult will it be to get a solid foothold in the market?

Market Share. What is the market size in total potential sales and what percentage of the market is shared by each competitor? Knowing the strengths and weaknesses of the competition, what percentage of the market can be captured by OPQ Supply company in one, two or three years.

Sales Potential. Project the sales that QRS Supply Company can achieve in the new market for the next one, two and three years. One method of projecting the sales is determining the total sales available in the market and the percentage of market share to be captured. Multiplying total sales by QRS Supply Company's percentage of market share to be captured equals the projected sales. Then, project the potential sales and market share for one, two and three years.

Human Resources. How many employees are required to service the market? Separate the staffing into office, and sales. Include the number of employees needed for one, two and three years and their respective incomes. This may first require reconstructing an organization chart to determine the functional needs for the expansion and subsequent staffing positions. If hiring within the new market, determine how strong the available job is pool and the average pay rates. This is necessary to project labor costs.

Physical Asset Resources. What facilities are needed, i.e. building, equipment, supplies, tools and work areas. Each asset category should include the approximate costs.

Marketing Resources What are the marketing and advertising costs necessary to implement the sales and marketing plan? The human, physical assets, and marketing resource costs are the total allocated resource costs.

Rate Bid or Quote. The type of invoicing and rate system that will be used and what profit margins will be awarded the service. Customer, competitors, and competitor's employees are resources used to determine the market's profit potential.

Market Direct Costs. Total the labor, materials and other direct costs. Divide the direct costs by the projected sales that are projected to determine the variable direct cost percent.

Market Overhead. What is the cost to operate the business in the location or expand the market? This includes the market's office administration (office and sales payroll, equipment, utilities, and so on) and the physical assets such as equipment costs, maintenance and repairs.

The question now arises as to what percentage of overhead costs should be applied to the new market. This can be based as a percentage of sales that the new market will add to the hotel. The percentage of business multiplied by the general overhead costs equals to the amount of overhead that is to be allocated to the new market.

Next is how much sales must be generated in the market just to pay for all the costs and expenses? The formula for determining breakeven is:

Fixed costs
100 - Variable Cost percent or

Market overhead + general overhead
100 - direct cost percent

Breakeven sales are compared to the sales projection to determine when the market will be able to stand on its own and begin to contribute profit to the company. Management wants to know how many months or years before breakeven is achieved.

Return on Investment. What will be the return of investment after one, two and three years? A pro forma income statement can be generated from the above information (sales - direct costs - market overhead - general overhead = profit). The assets necessary to establish the market are also known, Return on investment is the profit divided into the assets (at replacement value). This percentage displays the rate of return for each market expansion opportunity over a three-year period and answers the question, *Which opportunity provides the best return on the assets necessary for expansion?*

Risk: What is the risk of failure or margin of error in the market analysis? For simplification, determine how comfortable management is with the market analysis, and what the potential is for failure due to competition, economic conditions, or technological changes. This can be on a scale of 1(low risk) to 5 (high risk).

Funding Resources. How will the expansion be funded, i.e. profits, assets, financing or other outside resources? Obviously, if the expansion costs more than the available funding resources, the opportunity may be unfeasible. However, all potential funding resources should be considered.

Market Summary. When considering several expansion options, the marketing analysis can become difficult to evaluate on a comparative basis. A summary chart can be used to rate each option on a scale of one to five. (See chart at end of this section.) The marketing analysis provides the information necessary to rate somewhat objectively. The summary rating criteria are listed below.

COMPETITION. 1 = small or little competition, 5 = large or heavy competition.

MARKET SHARE POTENTIAL. 1 = excellent potential, 5 = low potential to attain significant market share.

RESOURCE ALLOCATION COST. 1 = low resource costs, 5 = high resource costs.

GROWTH POTENTIAL. 1 = high or fast sales growth potential, 5 = low or slow sales growth potential.

BREAKEVEN POINT. 1 = breakeven is achieved in no or very short time, 5 = breakeven is achieved in a long time.

RETURN ON INVESTMENT. 1 = high ROI, 5 = low ROI.

RISK. 1 = low risk potential, 5 = high risk potential.

Each rating category can be totaled to compare the marketing opportunities. Each category can be weighted according to importance. For example, return on investment may be more important than resource allocation cost if the funds are readily available; therefore, return on investment rating may be multiplied by a factor of 3, while resource allocation cost is multiplied by a factor of 1.

Marketing or determining growth options is not an exact science. Common sense guidelines and planning are the best tools for management to use in determining viable growth opportunities. This procedure provides a direction for determining the most viable options.

MARKET SUMMARY REPORT

Existing Markets

Marketing				

Concept				
Competition				
Market Share Potential				
Resource Allocation Cost				
Growth Potential				
Breakeven Point				
Return-on-Investment				
Risk				
Total:				

New Markets

Marketing Concept				
Competition				
Market Share Potential				

Resource Allocation Cost				
Growth Potential				
Breakeven Point				
Return-on-Investment				
Risk				
Total:				

Developing a Sales and Marketing Plan
For the purpose of this procedure, the following definitions provide a useful identification of concepts used in the marketing function.

Marketing: The identification of potential customers, and the presentation of a company and its products or services for the purpose of developing customer awareness of them.

Image: The perception the general public, business community and government have of your services. These factors affect patronage.

Advertising: Types of media information (in print, broadcast, video, or computer forms) that are specifically designed to encourage the selection of your services.

Promotion: The concentrated effect of presenting your services that are designed to encourage interest and increase repeat customers.

Target Marketing: A marketing concept of tailoring marketing efforts to a well-defined customer profile. Prospects must be selected on proven criteria such as type of business, size and location of business. This is the most cost-effective approach to marketing and provides the greatest return for our efforts and resources.

Selling: The end result of marketing, based on salesmanship. The specific actions involved in causing the customer to select our services and products. The sales employees are instrumental in this process.

The four P's: Product, presentation, pricing and promotion sum up a company's services, marketing and sales.

Basic marketing principles: Following are a few fundamental guidelines for companies with an established customer base:

Prevent loss of current customer base: This is the first rule in any approach to sales growth (we have to keep what we have!).

Cultivate key customers to reach others: These are customers who have been sold on our services and are repeat customers. Based on their trust they provide a "nest of referrals" for additional business.

Selectively acquire new accounts: It is a requisite for future growth that we have a plan to attract new customers on a selective basis such as target marketing.

Telemarket: The use of the telephone for promotion and follow-up with targeted customers and leads or referrals is historically the least expensive method of getting sales.

Sales and Marketing Plan: Purpose
Why should we develop a sales and marketing plan?

It gives us a track to run on.
It helps set specific targets towards which we aim.

It provides a means to measure success.

It prepares us for corrective action if we aren't reaching our targets.

It establishes a base for follow-up planning.

It pursues profitability.

What are the essential ingredients our company needs to make our sales and marketing plan successful?

Our services need to be oriented to our customers' needs and wants.

Our company needs to be effective in getting our services to the customer.

Our plan needs to identify strategies and responsibilities for implementing action programs to achieve the desired results.

A prime requisite for successfully managing the sales and marketing function is good information about the market and its potential. Frequently, a market research program conducted by company employees can disclose trends and problems. (Many times a questionnaire can be presented to current customers and prospects which can disclose trends and problems.) These trends and problems, in turn, can readily be addressed and provide vital data for our sales and marketing plan.

The most critical part of our plan is to organize our efforts for the fiscal year. The reason is that our sales and marketing plan is the means we will use to achieve the sales and profit projections developed in our forecast budget.

As with any process, there is a logical approach to the development of a sales and marketing plan. It must consider all resources available such as finances, resident talent, and community resources. Additionally, opportunities need to be defined and pitfalls identified. All during this process we need to be open to a marketing opportunity. Specifically, a marketing opportunity is an exploitable situation which we can turn into increased sales, profit or competitive edge through some marketing and/or sales action. Effective steps to building a plan are as follows:

Assess current and past sales and profits versus the marketing activity and expenses applied.

Assess company fiscal and operational goals.

Translate goals into sales & marketing objectives and strategies. Assess present sales & marketing skills and resources.

Develop measurement criteria and the methods to assess effectiveness.

After the above steps have been taken, the specifics can be developed and committed to paper, and then put into effect:

Formulate a plan.

Actualize the sales effort.

Assess success.

Review the plan. A sales and marketing plan involves identifying characteristics, values, and needs of prospective customers and addressing those through advertising, mailing, and networking, and selling. It is a tool that must be kept responsive to the evolving business population. In short, it must be updated regularly, perhaps on a quarterly basis.

Information fact base needed to prepare to draft a sales and marketing plan:

Sales -- historical

Markets

Trends

Service alternatives

Competition

Survey of customer attitudes

Methods for communicating with customers

Problems and opportunities

Discussion of objectives

Proposed strategy
        Conservative, optimistic
        Expected sales and profits
        Realistic budget

Probing questions that will help us determine our preferred approach to target marketing:

What is our marketplace?

Who are the significant users of our service?

Who are our major competitors?

How do we compare with our competitors?

How do we rate ourselves as a business?

What customer needs do we plan to fulfill?
To fulfill these needs, what must we change or continue to do well?

What skills and resources do we have?

What sales & marketing skills and tools did we have available last year to obtain the new business?

Have we installed sales quotas by product for each quarter consistent with resource planning?

What actions can we take to achieve our goals?

Have we established performance evaluation criteria?

What are our company goals?

What is the major customer market segment in our operating area?

What forms of salesmanship, promotion and advertising activities will we use to promote our products?

What accounts do we currently concentrate on and where should we expand?

Will we be able to get increased volume from current customers or the upgrading of marginal customers?

What type of prospecting will we use?

Whom will we target as potential customers?

What is our strategy for developing new accounts?

What actions will we take to achieve this strategy?

Is there sufficient capital available to accomplish our goals?
How will we measure the effectiveness of our activities?

Will we use sales call logs?

Will we use ratios of marketing/selling expense to sales?

Will we measure the number of new and/or repeat customers?

Will we use comparisons to prior years?

Typical Sales and Marketing Plan
       What follows is an outline of a written sales and marketing plan:

Executive Summary

Company Outlook
       The Firm
       The services
       Strengths

        Weaknesses
        Opportunities
        Threats

Market Status
        Industry
        Markets (by region and by availability of alternative
        transportation)
        Competition
        Substitution (of other transportation alternatives for our
        services)
        Key demand criteria
        Price analysis

Objectives and Strategies
        By market segment
        Target market
        Promotional programs
        Trade associations/ seminars
        Publicity
        Direct mail
        Advertising
        Internet

Sales Plan
        Forecast by market segment -- conservative, optimistic,
        expected
        Target customers
        Goals for current customer base

Organization
        Assigning responsibilities and timetables:
            Marketing
            Sales
            Sales & marketing support services

Other employees with substantial customer contact

Financial Results
      Objectives (overall financial intentions)
      Goals (Specific ending points)
      Plans (Steps to reach ending point)

After the sales and marketing plan has been committed to paper, we need to put it into effect. This requires us to identify priorities and set up sequential steps to carry out. From our planning, we should be aware of contingencies or obstacles we may encounter.

As we begin to carry out the plan, we must monitor it to make sure planned achievements are actually being attained. This requires that all sales efforts be quantified on a monthly and quarterly basis by establishing goals. We must review the results each month.

We need to analyze results to determine if and how our efforts are insufficient. Consider the following line of questions:

Are sales poor because the effort is poorly conceived and implemented?

Are sales poor because our business promotion lacks guidance from management?

Are we using the wrong marketing tools?

How can we modify our efforts to make them succeed?

What alternative methods could we try?

If we conclude that our efforts have been deficient, then employees training or changes are in order. If our results are deficient due to other circumstances, perhaps factors external to our company, then our plan needs to be amended and we need to continue with a well-structured and organized approach to sales & marketing.

A sales and marketing plan is of paramount importance to any company in business today. Whatever the industry, whatever the size, it is imperative that we assess where we stand, where we plan on going, and how we are going to get there.

Properly prepared and implemented, the company sales and marketing plan will guide us, and if followed, will keep us on track to achieve the company's goals and objectives.

Sample Sales and Marketing Plan Worksheet

EXECUTIVE SUMMARY:
(Presents a overview of the proposed sales and marketing plan)

_____

_____

_____

_____

CURRENT MARKET SITUATION:
(Present background information)

Current market and products

_____

_____

_____

_____

Competition Strengths

_____

_____

_____

Competition Weaknesses

Distribution

Business Environment

Opportunities and Issue Analysis

Main Opportunities

Company Strengths

_____
_____
_____
_____
_____

Threats or Weakness

_____
_____
_____
_____
_____

Issues facing the sale of products and services

_____
_____
_____
_____

Objectives:
(Defines the Goals and Objectives)

Sales volume by month:

January	_____
February	_____
March	_____
April	_____
May	_____
June	_____
July	_____
August	_____
September	_____
October	_____

November _____

December _____

Total _____

Market Share _____

Profit (by month)

January _____

February _____

March _____

April _____

May _____

June _____

July _____

August _____

September _____

October _____

November _____

December _____

Total Profit _____

Market Strategy:
(Presents the basic marketing approach to be used to achieve plan objectives)

By Market Segment.

_____

_____

_____

Target Market

_____

_____

_____

Promotional Programs:

Direct Mail

_____

_____

_____

Publicity _____

_____

_____

_____

Advertising

_____

_____

_____

_____

_____

Other programs (list)

_____

_____

_____

_____

_____

Trade
Shows/Seminars/Reception_____

_____

Action Programs
(Provides answers to key elements)

214

What will be done:

_____

_____

_____

_____

_____

Schedule - When will it be done:

_____

_____

_____

_____

_____

Who will do it:

_____

_____

How Much Will It Cost:

_____

_____

_____

_____

_____

Projected profit/loss
(Forecast the expected financial outcome from the plan and
assorted actions).

Projected profit/Loss _____

Controls
(Every element needs a means to be measured)
      Budgets
      Financial statements
      Schedules
      Other measurements

McCain's Maxim # 19: Don't forget this essential task when constructing a sales and marketing plan: Identify research trends in your product (or service) that will *change* the way products and services are used today. Then position your product or service accordingly, and take care to see if the industry leader is following suit. If it is, it's almost a sure sign you're on the right road.

CHAPTER NINETEEN

Analyze Your Business

Use the Analytical Tools and Checklists Described in This Chapter to Evaluate the Strength of Your business

Nothing in business is perfect, at least not for any sustained period. If it is perfect it doesn't stay that way for very long. Sooner or later problems develop. This chapter explores how the owner or manager of a small to medium-sized company starts: by asking the right questions and evaluating them as objectively as possible in four categories: money, activities, employees, and sales (MAPS: refer to Appendix for *Glossary of Terms used in MAPS*). This structured approach allows the analyst to focus on discovering the root causes of problems and points in the direction of solutions.

Money

A company unable to control its costs is a company quickly headed toward oblivion. The following checklist was designed to uncover weaknesses in costing, cost control, and other subjects related to reducing costs and maintaining a low cost operation.

Do you have long term cash planning to anticipate seasonal and capital requirements?

How do you anticipate and control cash flow in the short term, six weeks or less?

How do you anticipate and control cash flow in the short term, six weeks or less?

Do you have documented costing procedures in use?

How are units estimated tracked to purchasing?

How are "units" purchased tracked to units produced, shipped and invoiced?

Are your pricing procedures based on costing? How do you do it?

Does management receive timely reports of daily, weekly and monthly critical to success factors? From whom? When?

How many revenue streams do you identify? How many do you have?

Do you align direct costs with revenues streams?

What variance reporting do you have? Is it aligned with corrective action?

In-house management reporting of critical revenue and expense items should be available as part of information management to verify operations and finances. Are they?

Do you develop a profit forecast? How?

What process encourages employees to monitor and control expenses in their respective areas?

Have you a program to encourage streamlining operations and associated expenses?

Who, if anyone, constructs your zero-base budget? This is an excellent management training and communications building tool.

Are control reports nested by area to limit the span of control to elements significant in size and within individual control?

If job cost tracking applies, is it done? Does it affect customer billing? Employee incentives? Future bidding? Phase control?

When quotes are given, who validates the pricing? Does everyone capable of offering a price have the same training?

How do you test that they get the same results?

Are contracts reviewed before finalization to: assure our ability to perform? Have necessary resources available? Verify that vendors can comply?

Would it be beneficial to convert accounts payable into debt? What is the plan?

Are accounts receivable managed to comply with terms? With the company's ability to fund?

What strategy is in place for old accounts receivable?

How is credit granted? Is there a formal application and verification process? Are outside agencies used to confirm creditworthiness? Do you have personal guarantees for new accounts?

Is inventory managed to minimize investment and obsolescence while keeping up with customer demand? How?

Where does inventory appear on your daily and weekly report of finances?

Describe your inventory pricing matrix.

Who decides on issuing credits, returns, allowances, repairs?

What is the control? How much is spent (do not accept anything less than a hard number)? What is the tracking mechanism by customer, sales person, product, and so on?

What is done to safeguard gross margins in costing and pricing?

Is profit predetermined?

Who has authority to discount pricing? Why? To what limit?

Are overhead and labor burden properly calculated? How frequently? Can you demonstrate the worksheets?

How are overhead and labor burden controlled? To what extent are they included in your pricing model? How frequently are they revised? Can you show me the last two revisions?

Do you treat overhead as an accounting necessity or a marketing tool?

What are the measures of performance for the functions within the accounting and financial areas?

Which ratios do you use to help run your business? How are these communicated to the rest of the management group?

How many invoices do you send each day?

Do you have a purchasing control system in place?

How often do you evaluate your Worker's Comp and other insurance? When was the last audit? What was the result?

If you are subject to collection of Sales and Use Tax, have you ever undergone an audit? What was the result?

Does your current accounting system provide you with user friendly reports focused on the data you want to run your company?

How and how often do you review departmental costs with your department heads?

Activities

Measurement and control of performance standards is key to a successful company. Metrics, the application of meaningful numbers to track and control all aspects of operations, has been called the very heart of a company. The following list describes the questions to ask that will uncover how well your metrics are performing.

Do you have standards of performance for all key functions? Are they written?

How are the standards communicated?

What tracking mechanism follows the units of measure, standards and performance?

How are work and resources scheduled? How are responsibilities and authorities assigned?

Is a corrective action process in use? Demonstrate it.

Is preventive action part of management planning?

Do you have a continual improvement system? What is the quality policy supporting this system?

How do you prevent repeated failures of the same type?

Do you have a safety program? Risk management program?

If you ship, how many shipments do you make per week?

Do you have a process map of activities from initial customer contact, through operations and into sales and customer follow-up?

What worksheets do you use? Who uses them? Do they track all of your critical to success factors?

Do you assign projects with a plan for implementation by department?

Are your checklists of the phases of operation representative of your and customer requirements?

Do you have a strategic plan for long range planning? How is it communicated to your employees and business partners?

If you use subcontractors, do you follow a work management plan?

How are employees recognized and rewarded for exceeding company requirements?

What is your inspection process? Is it progressive and reviewed?

Do you have a final inspection procedure? What is found? How are non-conformities handled?

When is inventory reconciled? Are there discrepancies? To what extent? What action is taken?

Do you use a preventive maintenance system? How does it track?

Do you use a predictive maintenance system?

Are your checklists of the phases of operation representative of your and customer requirements?

How are customer orders tracked and kept moving toward fulfillment?

Who and by what mechanism are customers kept informed about their order status?

When there is a complaint how is it logged? What happens next?

What is the resource capacity per work unit?

Is there a limiting step or constraint preventing improvement?

People

What's more fundamental to the success of a company than the training and development of its people, from top to bottom of the company? This section asks the kind of questions that reveal the answer.

Do all of your positions have performance measures?

How do you anticipate and control cash flow in the short term, six weeks or less?

Do employees understand the importance of performance measures to themselves and the company?

What is your mission statement? How is it shared with employees?

Which individual departments have its own mission statement that is also consistent with the company outlook?

Do you have a training function? Is it formalized? Which departments are covered? Is on-going competency testing part of the training? Should it be?

What is your cross training practice? Do you have a skills matrix?

Is compensation pegged to performance measurables?

Do you use a pay scale? How was it determined?

Which managers have job descriptions specifying duties, responsibilities, authorities and measurable performance standards?

Are benchmarking systems in place for employees to measure their own progress and performance?

If tools are used by your employees, are they responsible for properly maintaining them? Who pays for replacements due to abuse?

Are you aligned with any government or union apprentice programs?

What is your formal recognition program for employees? Are incentives offered?

On what frequency are salaries reviewed? Is an evaluation required?

Do you use a follow-up system to verify that deficiencies uncovered during the evaluation are remedied?

Are training aids provided at the point where work is performed?

Do non-management/supervisory employees have task and duty lists with measurable performance indicators?

Where is your organization chart displayed? Is it meaningful in terms of representing the reporting relationships in the company?

Have you prepared a functional organization chart that identifies each function performed and the position responsible? Are all key functions shown? Does the functional assignment make best use of individual resources?

Sales

Sales and marketing, like their counterparts in operations and administration have certain minimum prerequisites that assure the dollars invested in these functions are being used to the fullest extent. The following checklist will help you evaluate how well it's being done.

Do all of your positions have performance measures?

How do you anticipate and control cash flow in the short term, six weeks or less?

Do employees understand the importance of performance measures to themselves and the company?

What is your mission statement? How is it shared with employees?

Which departments have their own mission statements that are also consistent with the company outlook?

Do you have a training function? Is it formalized? Which departments are covered? Is on-going competency testing part of the training? Should it be?

What is your cross training practice? Do you have a skills matrix?

Is compensation pegged to performance measurables?

Do you use a pay scale? How was it determined?

Which managers have job descriptions specifying duties, responsibilities, authorities and measurable performance standards?

Are benchmarking systems in place for employees to measure their own progress and performance?

If tools are used by your employees, are they responsible for properly maintaining them? Who pays for replacements due to abuse?

Are you aligned with any government or union apprentice programs?

What is your formal recognition program for employees? Are incentives offered?

On what frequency are salaries reviewed? Is an evaluation required?

Do you use a follow-up system to verify that deficiencies uncovered during the evaluation are remedied?

Are training aids provided at the point where work is performed?

Do non-management/supervisory employees have task and duty lists with measurable performance indicators?

Where is your organization chart displayed? Is it meaningful in terms of representing the reporting relationships in the company?

Have you prepared a functional organization chart that identifies each function performed and the position responsible? Are all key functions shown? Does the functional assignment make best use of individual resources?

Self-Assessment

The following pages show the MAP chart an owner or manager can use to assess his or her company. The items to measure are shown in the column on the left. They're marked in gray and include (1) quality management system, (2) management responsibility, (3) resource management, (4) product realization, and (5) measurement, analysis and improvement.

Note that the analyst has an opportunity to assess a score for each of the functions described in the left-hand column. The assessed scores run from zero to 100, with zero an absolute failure or not performed at all, and 100 the top possible score indicating excellence.

The first fifty scores means that the function is performed but without any accompanying written procedures and/or instructions. To land a score between 50 and 100 a written procedure is mandatory.

To get an idea of what a completed score sheet for a company looks like take a look at the chart following the MAP chart on the following page. It's titled *Sample Analysis Comparing Consultant's MAP Score with Client's MAP Score* and it demonstrates the difference between the scores made by an independent observer and the owner or manager of the business. Of course, the independent observer (consultant) brings his years of experience to the table along with his objectivity.

McCain's Maxim # 20: It's difficult for owners and managers to objectively analyze their businesses and point out their companies' weaknesses. Their

judgment can be clouded by lack of comparative experience, pride, and unwillingness to accept that their "Baby" is not perfect. That's where the judgment of an experienced independent consultant has its greatest value.

		Score	N/A	This is done, No Write Up											Requires Written Procedure									
				0	5	10	15	20	25	30	35	40	45	50	55	60	65	70	75	80	85	90	95	100
4.0	**Quality Management System**																							
4.1	General Requirements																							
4.2	General Documentation Requirements																							
5.0	**Management Responsibility**																							
5.1	Management Commitment																							
5.2	Customer Focus																							
5.3	Quality Policy																							
5.4	Planning																							
5.4.1	Quality Objectives																							
5.4.2	Quality Planning																							
5.5	Administration																							
5.5.1	General																							
5.5.2	Responsibility and Authority																							
5.5.3	Management Responsibility																							
5.5.4	Internal Communication																							
5.5.5	Quality Manual																							
5.5.6	Control of Documents																							
5.5.7	Control of Quality Records																							
5.6	Management Review																							
5.6.1	Review Input																							
5.6.2	Review Output																							
6.0	**Resource Management**																							
6.1	Provision of Resources																							
6.2	Human Resources																							
6.2.1	Assignment of Personnel																							
6.2.2	Training, Awareness & Competency																							
6.3	Facilities																							
6.4	Work Environment																							
7.0	**Product Realization**																							
7.1	Planning of Realization Processes																							
7.2	Customer-related Processes																							
7.2.1	Identification of Customer Requirements																							
7.2.2	Review of Product Requirements																							
7.2.3	Customer Communication																							
7.3.1	Design and/or Development																							
7.3.2	Design and/or Development Planning																							
7.3.3	Design and/or Development Inputs																							
7.3.4	Design and/or Development Outputs																							
7.3.5	Design and/or Development Review																							
7.3.6	Design and/or Development Verification																							
7.3.7	Design and/or Development Validation																							

		Score	N/A	This is done, No Write Up												Requires Written Procedure									
				0	5	10	15	20	25	30	35	40	45	50	55	60	65	70	75	80	85	90	95	100
7.4	Purchasing																							
7.4.1	Purchasing Control																							
7.4.2	Purchasing Information																							
7.4.3	Verification of Purchased Products																							
7.5	Production and Service Operations																							
7.5.1	Operations Controls																							
7.5.2	Identification and Traceability																							
7.5.3	Customer Property																							
7.5.4	Preservation of Product																							
7.5.5	Validation of Processes																							
7.6	Control of Measuring and Monitoring Devices																							
8.0	**Measurement, Analysis and Improvement**																							
8.1	Planning																							
8.2	Measurement and Monitoring																							
8.2.1	Customer Satisfaction																							
8.2.2	Internal Audit																							
8.2.3	Measurement and Monitoring of Processes																							
8.2.4	Measurement and Monitoring of Product																							
8.3	Control of Nonconformity																							
8.4	Analysis of Data																							
8.5	Improvement																							
8.5.1	Planning for Continual Improvement																							
8.5.2	Corrective Action																							
8.5.3	Preventive Action																							

SAMPLE ANALYSIS COMPARING CONSULTANT'S MAP
SCORE WITH CLIENT'S MAP SCORE

	Consultant	Client
MONEY		
Develop long term cash planning	20	40
Develop and install Management Control Accounting	100	300
Develop a Flash report modified for Revenue & Expense	40	140
ACTIVITIES		
Develop Standards of Performance for both plants	50	150
Devise a Recognition incentive program	25	75
Set measures of performance for office functions	25	50
Assist in developing a scheduling system	50	150
Install a Corrective Actions procedure	15	60
Establish a Safety program	40	160
Begin a Preventive Maintenance program on equipment	25	120
SALES		
Develop a Sales Planning and Control Process	30	125
Train Sales to calculate personal income & goals	10	50
Begin using video and audio training	5	75
Develop a Benefits profile for customers	10	100
Begin a program to solicit and penetrate corporate accts	10	60
Introduce a customer based forecasting system	30	180
Identify customer objections and prepare responses	15	35
Develop sales incentives rewarding accomplishments	10	20
Create a customer profile, calculate lifetime margin	15	80
Identify a Unique Selling Proposition	10	40
PEOPLE		
Develop performance measures for defined positions	60	125
Introduce performance measures and value to employers	10	30

CHAPTER TWENTY
Prepare a Succession Plan

It Provides Owners Peace of Mind

As a management consultant, working with many companies across the USA, I've had the opportunity to advise many company owners about the wisdom of preparing thorough succession plans, and then helping then construct such plans.

Every now and then I would hear a tragic story of how company founders and owners, all who sweat blood, sweat, and tears in the founding and nurturing of their companies (as precious to them as their own children), neglected to make succession provisions, and lost control of their destinies.

One example that stands out is the founder and owner of a small manufacturing company in the South. He had both a son and a daughter. The son, speaking frankly, was a spoiled brat who indulged in the pleasures of life but avoided the work and responsibilities that came with the family business. Thankfully his daughter was bright, hard working, and ambitious. He decided to pass ownership of the company to her and avoid including his son in any of his succession plans.

Before he had a chance to set up his succession plans, he had a stroke that left him comatose and on life support systems for several weeks, and then he died, without a succession plan in place.

The ownership of his company passed on to both his son and daughter. The daughter wanted to run the company; the son wanted to sell it to the highest bidder. A war ensued. While the siblings fought it out, the company slowly withered away without the guardianship it needed.

Long story short: The company died and went into receivership. Along with it, the founder's dream.

A closely-held corporation needs a succession plan as much as any other type of business. Stockholders and executives of a closely-held corporation are usually one and the same. When a stockholder dies, the corporation, unlike a partnership, continues its independent legal existence. The shares of a deceased stockholder are passed on to his or her estate. If no plans have been made for the sale of stock or for a management change, the death of a stockholder could cause a host of problems for the business, the surviving shareholders, and the heirs.

If the surviving shareholders own a majority of the stock, control of the business will not be affected. However, the business may sustain financial losses when the expertise of a key manager is lost. The heirs of a minority stockholder may complicate business affairs since heirs have the right to vote and demand information about the management and finances of the company.

These are just some of the possibilities a business may face if it is stranded without leadership in key functional areas. The consequences are serious, so it is important for any type of business to have a succession plan.

Your decision about who will take over your business when you leave will be one of the most important decisions of your career. It could mean the difference between the collapse of your business or its continuing success after you retire. This is a decision that calls for careful planning. You will need to make decisions about insurance, buy-sell agreements, your will, and other matters that affect how your business will continue.

The family owned business is an increasingly attractive career choice for the children of business owners. Consequently, more families intend to pass on the leadership of their business to multiple offspring.

The dilemma for the parents, of course, is to choose which sibling will actually take administrative control of the company. How do we choose one child over another? Too many parents want to believe that if they don't face the succession issue, it will somehow solve itself or go away. Others leave the decision to the children themselves – rationalizing that the children should make the call since they have to live with it. However, it is clear that you should pick a successor or a management team to replace you and decide how to prepare financially for the management transition.

The first step in determining a child's interest in the business is to *ask them*. Ask if he or she would be interested in running your business after you retire. You could plan to leave the majority interest in your company to this child in your will, as suggested by an attorney who handles family business cases. Other tangible assets, such as real estate, could be left to your other children. Often life insurance can cover the differences in the value of your assets so that all children are treated equally.

Family members with an active interest in managing the business can be issued voting stock. Those family members interested only in income from the business could receive non-voting stock.

If you want to pass on your business to your child, you need to be as objective as possible about his or her abilities to successfully manage the business. If the child seems to lack the enthusiasm, confidence or competence to run the business, consider hiring a professional manager on an interim basis while your child prepares for the top job.

Choosing Your Successor

Consider all family members and others as potential successors. Be as objective when you hire and promote relatives as you are when you manage and hire others. Use written job descriptions to guide your thinking when you consider the talents and limitations of possible successors.

Give positions and salaries to family members according to the company's needs and your relative's abilities. Try to avoid preferential decisions and salaries that favor relatives over other employees. Performance still must be the main criterion for success in your business.

Cultivate your heirs. They can work their way up the company ladder and be promoted on their personal merits and performances.

Be Prepared

In a family-run business, the owner generally wears many hats, including those of general manager, chief financial officer, and even clerk or worker. Top management bears most of the responsibility and may have difficulty delegating authority. And because working owners and managers often link their identity and self esteem to the business, they find it hard to think of retiring and relinquishing control.

You need time to train your successor, strengthen your management team and operations. You need to start now to prepare a plan before a crisis happens.

As the owner, you have a wealth of knowledge about your company's operations. Many owners store this wisdom in their memories. If you have not taken the time to formally write down this critical information, now is the time to do so. This is especially vital, if your employees have to carry on with the business in case you are disabled by a sudden illness or accident. Here are typical pieces of information:

Your financial statements for the past five years, including names, addresses and telephone numbers of the accountants who prepared the statements.

A brief description of your company's working capital situation, return on investment trends and operating rates.

Copies of flexible budgets, annual budgets, a breakeven analysis, and monetary variance reports.

Details of any other financial encumbrances such as liens and personal loans.

Copies of lease agreements and the company's financial obligations under those leases.

A list of your company's current and previous banking relationships. Include bank accounts, loan information, trust, investment, and the bank official responsible for each.

A copy of the most current business plan prepared to support your financing arrangements.

A list of all stockholders and number of shares owned.

A list of your insurance policies.

Employee compensation and employment tax information.

Benefit plans.

The dates your company was founded, the names of its key players, and the major events in the company's history.

A company organization chart.

Job descriptions for all key players.

A list of all employment and labor agreements.

A list of leases.

A list of all contracts.

A list of all lawsuits past and present and the outcome or status of each.

Buy-sell agreements. These can grant surviving stockholders ongoing control of the business and provide financial security for the deceased heirs. A buy-sell agreement is a key element to a successful succession plan. Lenders and investors often will ask to see the buy-sell agreement when considering loans and other financial commitments. This type of agreement enables either the stockholders or the corporation itself to buy stock at a predetermined price from a deceased stockholder's estate. Many buy-sell agreements are funded by life insurance policies (purchased by the corporation) on the lives of each shareholder through insurance brokers specializing in coverage for business clients. Generally these policies are written for the value of each stockholder's shares. The value of the policies should be adjusted annually to reflect the current value of the stock. Surviving shareholders or the corporation can be named as the insurance beneficiary. When the stockholder dies, the insurance proceeds can be used to buy back the shares from his or her estate in order to satisfy the buy-sell agreement.

Stock option plans. Stockholders may decide to use a stock option plan as an alternative to a buy-sell agreement in the succession plan. Stock options give the heirs of a deceased stockholder the first chance to buy the deceased held shares. If the heirs decided not to buy the stock, the shares may be sold to the other shareholders or to outsiders.

A list of parts and materials that are regularly purchased.

A list of major suppliers along with basic procedures for purchasing.

Inventory of all major pieces of production.

Quality standards.

A description of how your services are provided.

A list of major customers.

Present marketing geographical area.

A description of major competitors.

Names, addresses, and a brief description of outside professionals who work with your company. This would include bankers, accountants, attorneys, insurance brokers, and management consultants.

Heir Apparent

Rotate the heir apparent through jobs for which job descriptions have been written. Evaluate the performance of that person. The heir apparent could be a family member, a business associate, or somebody recruited.

Remember, training your heir apparent takes time. The two of you should share responsibility for solving business problems and making day-to-day decisions. As you groom your heir to take over the reins of the business, you should gradually hand over increasing responsibility for dealing with day-to-day operations.

Your chosen heir may prove unable or unwilling to take over the reins of the company. You must not be paralyzed and you might even have to start the whole process over again. Be prepared to face the jealousy many employees may exhibit towards the heir apparent. Key members of management may even leave the company after they realize their chance for advancement is blocked.

If there is not a clear heir apparent, or if you have to support an untrained heir, the team approach should be considered.

Work with several key members of the management team at once and look for the cream to rise. This allows you to build a little competition into the organization, and gives each candidate a chance to show me what you've got. As a side benefit, a pool of talent is developed from which to pick a successor at a later date, thus strengthening the entire organization.

Recruiting from the Outside

Carefully define your top management needs – your company's goals. Your operating, administrative and financial inventory will help you pull this together. The candidate from the outside should be shown a chance for advancement and an opportunity to work with you. Let him or her exercise a large degree of control over the job, and assure that this hand-selected heir have both a sense of accomplishment and a sense of security.

Training Your Successor

Training takes time. You may find yourself delaying business decisions while you explain them to your successor. Be fully aware that your successor may make mistakes that will cost money. Be prepared to act quickly to correct mistakes or clean up mistakes. Teach and train your successor to assure the same mistakes from the past are not repeated.

You may find delegating your authority, your work, and your responsibility to another person is one of the hardest jobs you will do. It is often very difficult to let go of control and responsibility when you have exercised them for a long time.

The key to all delegation is that you can only delegate to a *competent* person. The person filling a management spot needs to have, in addition to technical skills, the ability to plan, direct and coordinate the work of others. The manager's personality, initiative and leadership skills will also come into play.

Delegation will only work if you stand back and give your successor or manager the freedom to do things their way. Measure their performance by results, not how closely they emulate you.

There are a number of professionals you will need to help you plan for the future of your company as you cope with personal, legal, financial and tax issues. Here is a suggested list:

ACCOUNTANTS: To help you estimate tax liabilities, reduce your tax burden and establish an accurate value for your business. Accountants can also help you evaluate the financial impacts of retirement programs, trusts, compensation programs, benefit programs and other on-going expenditures.

ATTORNEYS: To draw up wills, buy-sell agreements, stock option plans, and to check the legality of your succession plan and other employees-related programs. An attorney experienced in estate planning and trust is also an excellent source of advice about succession plan alternatives.

BANKERS: To advise you about retirement savings plans and your company's finances, as well as trust, estate planning and pension planning.

INSURANCE BROKERS: To advise you about business succession plans, and your personal retirement plan. Since life insurance policies are the keystones of both these plans, the advice of an insurance broker experienced with life insurance and estate planning for business clients is vital.

MANAGEMENT CONSULTANTS: To advise you on how to build a strong management organization, how to inventory your company's strengths and weaknesses, and how to choose and train your executives. Management consultants may also advise you on how to structure management compensation and incentive programs.

TRUST OFFICERS: To help you establish a trust that will control the business on behalf of any minor heirs, or to act as a neutral third party to enforce a succession agreement such as a partnership agreement or a buy-sell agreement.

McCain's Maxim #21: Planning for management changes is an important part of your company's successful future. You have centered your life around your business for many years. It can be a painful personal experience to leave the work of a lifetime. However, parting is much easier if you know that your heirs have the tools necessary to carry on the tradition that you founded.

APPENDIX

Sample Mission Statements

My all-time favorite mission statement is actually a slogan by S.C. Johnson company for Raid. **Raid Kills Bugs Dead!**

These sample mission statements appear in alphabetical order. By looking at them it is easy to see that the formats are as different and diverse as the specific needs, ideology, and market conditions dictate.

3M sample mission statements

3M's commitment is to actively contribute to sustainable development through environmental protection, social responsibility and economic progress. To us, that means meeting the needs of society today, while respecting the ability of future generations to meet their needs.

Aquaya

To get clean water to poor people.

Anheuser-Busch sample mission statements

Be the world's beer company.
Enrich and entertain a global audience.
Deliver superior returns to our shareholders.

Barnes & Noble sample mission statements

Our mission is to operate the best specialty retail business in America, regardless of the product we sell. Because the product we sell is books, our aspirations must be consistent with the promise and the ideals of the volumes which line our shelves. To say that our mission exists independent of the product we sell is to demean the importance and the distinction of being booksellers

As booksellers we are determined to be the very best in our business, regardless of the size, pedigree or inclinations of our competitors. We will continue to bring our industry nuances of style and approaches to bookselling which are consistent with our evolving aspirations.

Above all, we expect to be a credit to the communities we serve, a valuable resource to our customers, and a place where our dedicated booksellers can grow and prosper. Toward this end we will not only listen to our customers and booksellers but also embrace the idea that the company is at their service.

Ben & Jerry's sample mission statements

Product Mission: To make, distribute & sell the finest quality all natural ice cream & euphoric concoctions with a continued commitment to incorporating wholesome, natural ingredients and promoting business practices that respect the Earth and the Environment.

Economic Mission: To operate the company on a sustainable financial basis of profitable growth, increasing value for our stakeholders & expanding opportunities for development and career growth for our employees.

Social Mission: To operate the company in a way that actively recognizes the central role that business plays in society by initiating innovative ways to improve the quality of life locally, nationally & internationally.

Central To The Mission Of Ben & Jerry's is the belief that all three parts must thrive equally in a manner that commands deep respect for individuals in and outside the company and supports the communities of which they are a part.

Caterpillar sample mission statements

Caterpillar will be the leader in providing the best value in machines, engines and support services for customers dedicated to building the world's infrastructure and developing and transporting its resources. We provide the best value to customers.

Caterpillar people will increase shareholder value by aggressively pursuing growth and profit opportunities that leverage our engineering, manufacturing, distribution, information management and financial services expertise. We grow profitably.

Caterpillar will provide its worldwide workforce with an environment that stimulates diversity, innovation, teamwork, continuous learning and improvement and rewards individual performance. We develop and reward people.

Caterpillar is dedicated to improving the quality of life while sustaining the quality of our earth. We encourage social responsibility.

Charles Schwab

To help everyone be financially fit.

Chevron

Providing energy products and services that are vital to society's quality of life.

Being known as people with superior capabilities and commitment, both as individuals and as an organization.

Thinking and behaving globally, and valuing the positive influence this has on our company.

Being the partner of choice because we best exemplify collaboration.

Delivering world-class performance.

Earning the admiration of all our stakeholders—investors, customers, host governments, local communities and our employees—not only for the goals we achieve but how we achieve them.

Dow Chemical

To constantly improve what is essential to human progress by mastering science and technology.

Ford

We are a global family with a proud heritage passionately committed to providing personal mobility for people around the world.

We anticipate consumer need and deliver outstanding products and services that improve people's lives.

Gap

At Gap Inc. we never stop moving. It takes thousands of passionate, dedicated and talented employees around the world to deliver the merchandise and shopping experience our customers expect and deserve.

Google sample mission statements

To organize the world's information and make it universally accessible and useful.

Hershey Company sample mission statements

Undisputed Marketplace Leadership.

Top-tier value creation, driven by superior performance across the business system.

Organizational capabilities and passion that compete in the present and build for the future.

Commitment to enabling and encouraging balanced, healthy lives.

Portfolio of brands that:
- Delights consumer across multiple segments
- Delivers superior growth and profitability to retailers
- Is available everywhere

Ability to transform consumer and customer desires to marketplace wins.

HONDA

Maintaining a global viewpoint, we are dedicated to supplying products of the highest quality, yet at a reasonable price for worldwide customer satisfaction.

IBM sample mission statements

At IBM, we strive to lead in the invention, development and manufacture of the industry's most advanced information technologies, including computer systems, software, storage systems and microelectronics.

We translate these advanced technologies into value for our customers through our professional solutions, services and consulting businesses worldwide.

ING

We lead Americans back to savings

Johnson & Johnson sample mission statements

At Johnson & Johnson there is no mission statement that hangs on the wall. Instead, for more than 60 years, a simple, one-page document – Our Credo – has guided our actions in fulfilling our responsibilities to our customers, our employees, the community and our stockholders. Our worldwide Family of Companies shares this value system in 36 languages spreading across Africa, Asia/Pacific, Eastern Europe, Europe, Latin America, Middle East and North America. The English version of the Credo is below, or you may choose to view it in another language by selecting a country from the box on the right. You can also learn more about the history of Our Credo and its development.

Our Credo:

We believe our first responsibility is to the doctors, nurses and patients, to mothers and fathers and all others who use our products and services. In meeting their needs everything we do must be of high quality. We must constantly strive to reduce our costs in order to maintain reasonable prices. Customers' orders must be serviced promptly and accurately. Our suppliers and distributors must have an opportunity to make a fair profit.

We are responsible to our employees, the men and women who work with us throughout the world. Everyone must be considered as an individual. We must respect their dignity and recognize their merit. They must have a sense of security in their jobs. Compensation must be fair and adequate, and working conditions clean, orderly and safe. We must be mindful of ways to help our employees fulfill their family responsibilities. Employees must feel free to make suggestions and complaints. There must be equal opportunity for employment, development and advancement for those qualified.

We must provide competent management, and their actions must be just and ethical.

We are responsible to the communities in which we live and work and to the world community as well. We must be good citizens – support good works and charities and bear our fair share of taxes.

We must encourage civic improvements and better health and education. We must maintain in good order the property we are privileged to use, protecting the environment and natural resources.

Our final responsibility is to our stockholders. Business must make a sound profit. We must experiment with new ideas. Research must be carried on, innovative programs developed and mistakes paid for. New equipment must be purchased, new facilities provided and new products launched. Reserves must be created to provide for adverse times. When we operate according to these principles, the stockholders should realize a fair return.

Ken Blanchard Companies sample mission statements

To unleash the potential and power of people and organizations for the common good.

McGraw-Hill sample mission statements

To provide essential information and insight that help individuals, markets, and societies perform to their potential.

Merck sample mission statements

The mission of Merck is to provide society with superior products and services by developing innovations and solutions that improve the quality of life and satisfy customer needs, and to provide employees with meaningful work and advancement opportunities, and investors with a superior rate of return.

Microsoft sample mission statements

To enable people and businesses throughout the world to realize their full potential.

Nike

To bring inspiration and innovation to every athlete in the world.

Pfizer sample mission statements

We dedicate ourselves to humanity's quest for longer, healthier, happier lives through innovation in pharmaceutical, consumer, and animal health products.

Proctor & Gamble sample mission statements

We will provide branded products and services of superior quality and value that improve the lives of the world's consumers. As a result, consumers will reward us with leadership sales, profit, and value creation, allowing our people, our shareholders, and the communities in which we live and work to prosper.

Ritz-Carlton sample mission statements

The Credo:

The Ritz-Carlton Hotel is a place where the genuine care and comfort of our guests is our highest mission.

We pledge to provide the finest personal service and facilities for our guests who will always enjoy a warm, relaxed, yet refined ambience.

The Ritz-Carlton experience enlivens the senses, instills well-being, and fulfills even the unexpressed wishes and needs of our guests.

Motto:

At The Ritz-Carlton Hotel Company, L.L.C., "We are ladies and gentlemen serving ladies and gentlemen." This motto exemplifies the anticipatory service provided by all staff members.

Sears sample mission statements

To grow our business by providing quality products and services at great value when and where our customers want them, and by building positive, lasting relationships with our customers.

Skype

To be destructive but in the cause of making the world a better place.

Smith International

Our people and technology make us a world leader in drilling tools and services. We work together to constantly improve customer satisfaction, employee opportunity and shareholder value.

Sony

To emotionally touch and excite our customers.

Southwest Airlines

The mission of Southwest Airlines is dedication to the highest quality of Customer Service delivered with a sense of warmth, friendliness, individual pride, and company Spirit.

To Our Employees:

We are committed to provide our Employees a stable work environment with equal opportunity for learning and personal growth. Creativity and innovation are encouraged for improving the effectiveness of Southwest Airlines. Above all, Employees will be provided the same concern, respect, and caring attitude within the organization that they are expected to share externally with every Southwest Customer.

Starbucks

Establish Starbucks as the premier purveyor of the finest coffee in the world while maintaining our uncompromising principles while we grow.

Xerox sample mission statements

Our strategic intent is to help people find better ways to do great work -- by constantly leading in document technologies, products and services that improve our customers' work processes and business results.

Yahoo sample mission statements

Our mission is to be the most essential global Internet service for consumers and businesses. How we pursue that mission is influenced by a set of core values - the standards that guide interactions with fellow Yahoos, the principles that direct how we service our customers, the ideals that drive what we do and how we do it. Many of our values were put into practice by two guys in a trailer some time ago; others reflect ambitions as our company grows. All of them are what we strive to achieve every day.

Glossary of Terms Used in MAPS

(See Chapter Nineteen)

Section	Term	Definition
People	Bench-marking	Setting an identifiable and measurable standard, typically of performance. Benchmarks can be used for continual improvement of individuals, processes, systems and companies.
Activities	Constraint	A limit affecting the ability of a system to increase throughput. The limit could be a physical, financial, personal, and measuring or policy condition.
Sales	Continual Improvement	An unending series of activities intended to improve a process or series of processes. The successful accomplishment of progressive actions to improve results.
Activities	Corrective Action	Action taken to remedy an existing condition. The action may provide temporary or permanent relief. It may also result in a procedure for handling recurring and non-preventable problems.

Activities	Critical to Success Factors	Factors necessary for the enterprise to survive and thrive. These factors may be independent such that the absence of any one is terminal to the system or interdependent meaning that they must exist in a dynamic balance.
Sales	CRM	Customer Resource Management systems track all customers marketing, sales and contact information. It provides a database for a company interested in keeping track of its customers without losing key data should a customer service or sales person leave the company.
Sales	Customer Profile	Contains background information that is personal and business. The type of business, its clients, size by sales and employees, purchases, related consumables, margins, location, and affiliations.
Activities	GAP Analysis	An assessment of current realities (practices) and best practices. The analysis typically takes from two to five days and produces specific recommendations for improvement, a plan of action, illustrated bottom line results, and a schedule for implementation.
Money	Labor Burden	All of the non-payroll costs of employment. These include taxes, insurance, benefits, uniforms, allowances, vacations, holidays, paid time off, and education assistance. Labor

		burden must be recaptured in order for a company to perform work profitably
Sales	Market Tracks	These are a series of marketing events used to woo and retain customers. One track might be used with suspects (targeted potential customers who have not made any overtures to buy); prospects (potential customers who have expressed interest); customers and non-purchasing customers. For example, on a track for a prospect you might send out a mass mailing, a few weeks later and secondary mailing, then a sample, then a phone call followed by an email, each at a pre-defined interval.
People	Metrics	Metrics are measures. The metrics are quantifiable and may be in any type of unit that is directly attributable to the process being measured: dollars, pieces, pounds, liters, ounces, feet, and so on.
People	Mission Statement	A statement of the company's direction and commitment to its fulfillment. It should contain an explanation of the mission and how to recognize progress toward it.
Activities	Non-conformities	Any product, service, event or act that does not conform to the stated and agreed requirements.

Money	Overhead Absorption	The amount and technique for capturing the fixed costs of a business into the costing and pricing formulas. Overhead may be absorbed over any number of different bases including dollars, units, employees, space, material, divisions or departments. When used with GSM pricing models, overhead absorption becomes a variable once pre-planned profit is instituted. Overhead must be fully absorbed within a period. Under absorption reduces profit and could result in a loss. Over absorbed overhead produces additional profit.
Money	Phase Control	Construction, manufacture, even paperwork occurs in a series of steps or processes. Where practical, a control mechanism should be placed along the path to help assure that the process is proceeding as planned and, if it is not, to provide early warning for corrective action.
Activities	Predictive Maintenance	Maintenance determined by historic failure tracking or through anticipation by direction intervention. For example, rather than have a belt break on a car engine then driver could check the belt's condition regularly and have it replaced when either a specific wear characteristic is seen or when it passes its defined useful life. In this manner downtime can be planned for natural production valleys instead of unexpectedly.

Activities	Preventive Action	Steps taken in anticipation of the possibility of a problem which institute action to prevent a harmful event.
Money	Pricing Matrix	A table with predefined conditions for setting prices based on cost. Typically, five pricing levels are used. The lowest cost category, say below $1, might have a 3.0 multiplier. Then, from $1 to $5 a 2.5 multiplier and so forth. The multiplier decreases as the cost of the item increases reflecting the increased dollar per unit profit realized. By weighting the volume in each category you calculate the effective gross margin for the entirety and by varying the multipliers you can achieve a specified margin. Be careful to pay attention to those commonly known items so that they are not charged in excess of common market knowledge.
Money	Process	An activity that works on an input and adds value in the creation of an output.
Activities	Process Map	A graphic illustration of the sequence of activities and decisions for a system.
Activities	Quality Needs Assessment	This 50 hour assessment evaluates the client's current business system against an international standard. The resulting summery report identifies cost of quality elements, the actions needed to remedy, and an estimate of the hours required. In addition, the client is also provided with identification of the specific non-conforming conditions for each specific

		point of the standard that is not being met.
People	Quality Statement	A statement of the company's commitment to quality with a clear definition of the factors used in defining quality for the company, it's employees, customers and supply chain.
Activities	Resource Capacity	The rate of output capable from each resource assuming there was no constraint or downtime on the system. It is an optimum. From this and the process flow we can seek to optimize the overall system by exploiting the constraints and making all other resources subordinated to it. For example, if a particular activity is capable of 12 work units an hour and is the slowest of all the activities, then overall throughput is governed by that activity. All other activities need less support and the slowest activity must be put in a position where it never slows or stops.
Money	Retain age	Primarily a contractor related term, retain age is an amount withheld from disbursement until the work is satisfactorily complete.

Activities	Risk Management	Insurance and safety areas relate through this concept. All business is subject to risk. Sometimes the risk is loss of labor time, investment funds, safety of assets and so forth. Business attempts to reduce risk exposure while maximizing opportunities for reward. Insurance provides a mechanism for accepting exposure to higher levels of risk with a safety net in the event that loss in incurred. While insurance reduces the immediate effect of loss, losses will increase premiums to recoup. Consequently, it is in the businesses best interest to assess the nature of potential loss and install safeguards.
People	Rubric	Self training and accepting responsibility for actions and outcomes can be anticipated and encouraged through use of rubrics. Essentially, this is a matrix of tasks and possible outcomes. The outcomes are weighted and apply to each of the actions expected through use of the rubric. For example, when creating task and duty lists, each task could be a line item and the various measures applicable to all of the tasks could be: requires constant supervision, requires less than 50% supervision, can work independently and is capable of training others. Each level of proficiency denotes increasing ability and sets a path for the individual to follow to recognize his or her own level of competency. When tied to a skills matrix and pay scale, the

		individual can track performance to the next pay grade with full knowledge of the expectations for each skill and level.
People	Skills Matrix	Delineates the various skills valued in the position, degrees of competency and, here applicable, pay grade. The matrix is often used to encourage cross training within a company or department.
Money	System	Systems are collections of processes. Just as each process results in output, the system results in throughput. Changes to processes and systems that do not increase throughput (for our clients this means dollars of profit) typify a waste of money and effort that could have been better spent on activities that affects the bottom line.
Sales	Unique Selling Proposition	Distinguishing benefits inherent in the product or service, which are claimed to set it apart from the competition.

Activities	Unit of Measure	Central elements of a system without any of the other components of the system. The central theme could be a component, even a relatively minor component, that is essential and a direct indicator of production. In a metal fabricating shop the central item could be the steel, in a restaurant the food. Remove either of these central elements and there is no longer any need for the remaining business functions.
Activities	Variance	All systems vary. Variance is the difference between a standard and the result. Variance outside of a predetermined level, set by either percentage or an absolute amount, requires corrective action. Positive variance should be encouraged and adverse variance either eliminated or controlled.
Sales	Worth of a Customer	A typical customer will have identifiable characteristics useful when setting sales, margin and sales commission goals. Understanding the longevity of the customer relationship, the amount and frequency of purchases, as well as the gross margin percentage, allows construction of a customer profile and the summation of margin created for a new, typical customer. Once known, the worth estimate will help determine a budget for obtaining and maintaining customers.

Money	Zero-base Budget	Based on optimization principles, the sera base budget is a high form of management training, team building and financial and operational planning. Once the chart of accounts is properly delineated to identify each revenue stream and its aligned expenses, each operations and financial area of the company contributes input for answering a series of four questions which are applied to every account in the chart of accounts. Note that all accounts, Revenue, Expense, Asset, Liability and Equity are included. The questions are: 1. Is the consequence of the elimination of this account too terrible for the enterprise to bear? If the answer is no, eliminate it; if the answer is yes, then ask 2) Is the application of this element too terrible for the enterprise to bear at X% of the current level, where X can vary from one percent to 200%. (This sets a number consistent with the activity level of the business). Question three asks whether the item can be provided from a different source and question four asks whether the price paid or received should be at a different level. All answers must be based on fact.
		The major shortcoming of this type of budget is that the first draft is based upon the preceding period's sales level and that future projections require preparation of a proper sales budget.

Summary of Author and His Previous Book

Dr. James (Jim) McCain, The Business Doctor ◆ Business Works ◆ http://www.bizdrsolution.com/ 541 Waite Road ◆ Rexford, NY 12148 ◆ 518-383-3337 ◆ *jim@bizdrsolution.com*

Jim McCain
Ph.D.
The
Business Doctor

Founder and
Owner of
Business Works

HOW *BUSINESS WORKS* CAN HELP THE TRADES CONTRACTOR

Business systems

Business Products

Consulting Services

Business Documents

Business Procedures

WHY TRADE CONTRACTORS FAIL AND HOW TO PREVENT IT
Thirty Years Helping Small Businesses Survive and Prosper

**A Book by
Jim McCain**

Jim McCain, *The Business Doctor*, founder and CEO of Business Works, packs his book with tips and techniques that will resolve your business problems and get your trades contracting company up and running in record time with record results.

He has earned his title *The Business Doctor*. During his career Jim consulted with almost 450 companies such as yours, many of them trades contractors . . . and has solved complex and intractable problems that otherwise would have bankrupted their businesses.

Jim's clients know he can get the job done:

"The most important aspects of your consulting work were in the areas of measuring performance, with a revised review process which will address the accountability issues. Effective budgets and their use will be a big improvement. We are satisfied that the recommendations and actions will allow us to tackle the main issues." KB, President Plumbing, Heating and Air Conditioning Supply Company Selkirk, NY

"I am writing at the conclusion of the work completed by Jim McCain. I feel that the analysis of my company was thorough and complete in developing an accurate financial picture of my company. The services I received will allow me to better understand the true costs of running my business. We are satisfied with the work completed." SPB Landscaping, Design and Maintenance Company Cohasset, MA

**Who Am I (The Business Doctor), and What Makes
Me an Expert in Helping Business Owners and
Managers? The Following Ad from My brochure
Says It All:**"Are your business problems more complex?
Do they require a deep background in functional
business problem-solving? BUSINESS WORKS CEO
Dr. Jim McCain, a 30-year veteran with over 450
satisfied business clients, provides general business
consulting. Contact the Business Doctor today for a free
two-hour business physical."

Here's my bottom line: I help companies solve business
problems. **I specialize in working with small to midsized
companies in a variety of manufacturing and service
businesses**. A few of my accomplishments include:

☐ Saved a tire company $146,000 in its first year operating
costs by reducing waste in man hours, inventory, and
vehicle maintenance.

☐ Responsible for a landscaping design and maintenance
company return to profitability.

☐ Prevented corporate bankruptcy for a $1.5 million laser
saw company by applying financial controls and
accurate job costing procedures.

☐ Assisted a $10 million per year emergency power
service provider with the implementation of sales
reporting, labor burden calculations, job descriptions,
incentive plans, and human resource procedures. The
company later grew to just over $100 million in sales
volume.

My website *Business Works*
http://www.bizdrsolution.com/ has proven to be an invaluable
aid to small business owners and managers. From there,

business owners and managers have downloaded literally thousands of business manuals, employee manuals, business plan templates, employee evaluation forms, and a host of other important business documents tailored to their individual businesses.

For 15 years, during my early career, I was a professor at the State University of New York (SUNY). During that time I wrote for many business publications and was a frequently sought-after speaker at local, national, and international meetings.

www.ingramcontent.com/pod-product-compliance
Lightning Source LLC
Chambersburg PA
CBHW031922190326
41519CB00007B/386